[brief]

[brief]

**make a bigger impact
by saying less ◄**

Joseph
McCormack

WILEY

Published by John Wiley & Sons, Inc., Hoboken, New Jersey.

Published simultaneously in Canada.

For general information on our other products and services or for technical support, please contact our Customer Care Department within the United States at (800) 762-2974, outside the United States at (317) 572-3993 or fax (317) 572-4002.

Wiley also publishes its books in a variety of electronic formats. Some content that appears in print may not be available in electronic formats. For more information about Wiley products, visit our web site at www.wiley.com.

Library of Congress Cataloging-in-Publication Data:

ISBN: 9781394324323 (paperback)

ISBN: 9781118704967 (cloth)

ISBN: 9781118705285 (ePub)

ISBN: 9781118705568 (ePDF)

Cover Design: Megan Palicki

Author Photo: courtesy of the Author

SKY10086705_100324

This is dedicated to Julie, my beloved wife.
Thank you for loving me and inspiring me every day.
Your presence in my life is a great gift.

CONTENTS

Foreword   *xiii*

Acknowledgments   *xv*

Preface   *xvii*

Part ONE
AWARENESS: HEIGHTENED AWARENESS
IN A WORLD BEGGING FOR BRIEF   1

1 *Why Brevity Is Vital*   *3*

Get to the Point or Pay the Price   3

Executive—Interrupted   5

Who's Responsible for Adapting When the Message Is Not
    Being Heard?   9

Timing Is of the Essence   9

BRIEF Balance: The Harmony of Clear, Concise, and
    Compelling   10

A BRIEF Timeout   11

2 *Mindful of Mind-filled-ness*   *13*

Brevity Is Like an Instant Stress Release   13

Battling Overcapacity   14

1. Information Inundation—The Water's Rising   15

2. Inattention—The Muscle Is Weakening   17

3. Interruption—The Rate Is Alarming   19

4. Impatience—The Ice Is Thinning   21

What Does It All Mean?   22
Your New Reality: There's No Time for a Slow Buildup   22
Test Yourself   24
Examination of Brevity   24
A New Professional Standard   25

3 *Why You Struggle with Brevity: The Seven Capital Sins*   **27**

Why Is It So Difficult?   27
1. Cowardice   28
2. Confidence   29
3. Callousness   29
4. Comfort   30
5. Confusion   31
6. Complication   31
7. Carelessness   32

4 *The Big Bang of Brevity*   **35**
A Success Story   35

Part **TWO**
DISCIPLINE: HOW TO GAIN DISCIPLINE
TO BE CLEAR AND CONCISE   41

5 *Mental Muscle Memory to Master Brevity*   **43**
The Exercise of Brevity   43

6 *Map It: From Mind Mapping to BRIEF Maps*   **45**
Your 11th Grade English Teacher Was Right   45
An Outline Is Missing, and So Is the Sale   47
Mind Mapping and the Modern Outline   49

BRIEF Maps: A Practical Tool for Delivering Brevity   51
How a BRIEF Map Can Be Used   52
Wrong Approach: Bob Chooses to Share but Not to Prepare   52
Right Approach: Bob Prepares a BRIEF Map and Maintains
   Executive Support   53
BRIEF Maps: What's the Payoff?   57

7 *Tell It: The Role of Narratives*   *59*

I'm Tired of Meaningless and Meandering Corporate
   Jargon. I'm Ready for a Good Story   59
Where's the Disconnect? When a Story Is Missing   62
The Birth of Narrative Mapping: A Way to Organize and
   Deliver Your Story   64
Rediscovery of Narratives and Storytelling: Breaking
   through the Blah, Blah, Blah   66
Listen, I'm Ready for a Story   67
Think About Your Audience: Journalism 2.0 and the
   Elements of a Narrative   69
Narrative Map (De)constructed   75
Seeing and Hearing Is Believing: The Story of the Evolution
   of Commerce   76

8 *Talk It: Controlled Conversations and TALC Tracks* *81*

Risky Business Trip   82
Controlled Conversations Are a Game of Tennis, Not Golf   84
TALC Tracks—A Structure for Balance and Brevity   84
Be Prepared for Anything   86
Audience, Audience, Audience   88

9 *Show It: Powerful Ways to Make a Picture Exceed a
Thousand Words*   *91*

Show-and-Tell: Which Would You Choose?   91
You Can See the Shift   92
Seeing Supersedes Reading   93

A Visual Language 94
Connect an Image with Your Story 96
Momentary Magic: Infographics in Business 97
Breakdown of Complex Information 98
The Age of YouTube and Business 99
TL; DR: Too Long; Didn't Read 101

10 *Putting Brevity to Work: Grainger and the Al and Betty Story* **105**

Part THREE

DECISIVENESS: GAINING THE DECISIVENESS TO KNOW WHEN AND WHERE TO BE BRIEF 111

11 *Meeting You Halfway* **113**
Defeat the Villains of Meetings 113
Meeting Villain #1: Time 114
Meeting Villain #2: Type 115
Meeting Villain #3: Tyrants 116
Change the Format and Tone—Make It a Conversation 118
Put BRIEF Back into a Briefing 119

12 *Leaving a Smaller Digital Imprint* **123**
The Digital Flood 123
BRIEF Hall of Fame: Verne Harnish 126
From Social Media to Venture Capital 128
Social Media Squeeze 130

13 *Presenting a Briefer Case* **133**
Practicing What You Preach 133
The Discipline of Brevity 134

Putting the Power Back in PowerPoint   138
Training as a TED Talk   139

14 *Trimming Your Sales (Pitch)*   143

Shut Up and Sell   143
Billboard on a Bumper Sticker   144
Time to Be Convincing and Concise   146
Cut to the Customer's Chase   149

15 *Whose Bright Idea Was That Anyway?*   153

Your Big Idea   153
A Mission-Critical Narrative   154
Clear Picture with Radical Focus   157
The Entrepreneur's Dilemma: Mixed Messages   158
Tailor Your Pitch to Your Investor's Needs   161

16 *It's Never Really Small Talk*   165

Brevity as a Conversational Life Raft   165
Momentary Misgivings Stall Momentum   166
Walk the Walk; Talk the Talk   168

17 *Help Wanted: Master of Brevity*   173

Not the Time for Anxious Rambling   173
Let Others Lead the Conversation   175
Talking Your Way out of a Job Offer   177

18 *I've Got Some Good News*   183

Pay the Favor of Brevity Forward   183
Let the Brilliance Shine Through   184
Speak the Language of Success   186
Get into the Habit of Saying, "Thank You"   187

19 *And the Bad News Is...*   *189*

The Bright (and Brief) Side of Bearing Bad News   189
Give It to Them Straight   190
Serving up the S#&$ Sandwich   192

20 *Got-a-Minute Updates*   *197*

The "Say-Do" Ratio   197
Be Prepared to Be Lean and Drive Out Wasteful Words   199
The Most Important Question: Why Am I Here?   204

Part **FOUR**

BEING BRIEF SUMMARY AND ACTION PLAN   207

Resources   *219*

Notes   *221*

About the Author   *225*

Index   *227*

FOREWORD

When Joe asked me to write the foreword, I was literally in the middle of wrapping up my own book (*Scaling Up*) and I thought I couldn't do it.

I wanted to do something special (and brief!) and you know how hard it is to say something brief. Then, I changed my mind.

Read the book.

You're busy; we all are.

Be a master of brevity. Now get started.

—Verne Harnish, Founder and CEO of Gazelles

ACKNOWLEDGMENTS

When I first told my kids that I was writing a book called *BRIEF*, the jokes started flying. You could only imagine their comments. My friends and extended family followed suit saying the book should be only 10 pages long.

Funny ... I'm still laughing.

All kidding aside, I want to thank all of them for their constant love and support. It has been wonderful to see their nonstop encouragement.

As for my coworkers, clients, and close collaborators, this book has given me a unique opportunity to have deeper conversations and start to dream with them about the possibilities of a "less is more" world. On many occasions, they have taken time from their day job to lend me a hand. In particular, Johnny, Angelo, Angela, and Megan have been invaluable to get *BRIEF* airborne.

There are a few people, Meghan and Joyce at Sheffield and Christine Moore at John Wiley & Sons, whom I have depended on throughout with an honest editorial push to omit needless words and make this a better book.

Regarding my current and former clients, I have shared their insights, commentary, successes, and failures all while respecting their confidentiality and excluding any sensitive information they have shared with me. In particular, I have changed some first names and omitted surnames of those serving in our country's Special Operations community.

Finally, for all of those that I have interviewed for this book—a heartfelt thank you. Truly, this is a topic that affects us all.

PREFACE

Why BRIEF?

In our attention-deficit economy, being brief is what's desperately needed and rarely delivered.

When we fail to be clear and concise, the consequences can be brutal: wasted time, money, and resources; decisions made in confusion; worthy ideas rejected; people sent off in wrong directions; done deals that always seem to stall.

As the founder of a boutique marketing agency that helps clients such as Harley-Davidson, BMO Harris Bank, MasterCard, and W. W. Grainger get their stories straight, I know this is a rare skill.

For years, business and military leaders have complained to me about the same things. Mixed messages keep missing the mark. People are not on the same page. Long-winded presentations go nowhere.

For businesses to succeed in an information-laden and hyperbusy economy, the rambling has to stop. So I decided to write BRIEF, a step-by-step approach to get to the point quickly.

Anyone can learn how to make what's complex clear. After my firm was in business for just a few years, I was invited to develop an original curriculum for U.S. Special Operations Command in Fort Bragg, North Carolina. It turned out that some of the most elite members of our military were weak communicators. They admitted their mission-critical briefs were painfully long, buried in details, and impossible to decipher.

The transformative work with Special Operations was—and still is—incredibly rewarding. That's how BRIEF was born. It's about lean communication. It's like Six Sigma for your mouth.

After a few days in our Narrative Mapping courses, I saw an immediate shift. They were able to leverage storytelling skills and BRIEF techniques to be clear and compelling when explaining complex missions. They delivered complicated information efficiently and effectively, with clearer context and more compelling explanations. They used fewer PowerPoint presentations. As a result, the leaders fostered better and more engaging conversations.

One of the participants commented, "The difference is dramatic. Our briefs can prove that less is more."

I believe the lessons learned with U.S. Special Operations can be used in the corporate world by those who want to be concise and clear when sharing their story.

You're busy, so I've designed the book to be immediately useful. If you read and follow along actively, you will learn to create clarity and meaning and drive out waste and confusion.

The book is organized around a new form of ADD: awareness, discipline, and decisiveness.

Part One: Awareness—the conviction to hold yourself and others to a higher standard of succinctness

Part Two: Discipline—the BRIEF approach to producing the mental muscle memory necessary to make you a lean communicator every time

Part Three: Decisiveness—the ability to recognize key moments when you need to convey what really matters effectively and efficiently

[brief] **BITS**

[LOCKED AND LOADED!]

Brevity is a choice.

When you want to get more, decide to say less. Those who want to succeed—even thrive—in an attention-deficit economy are masters of lean communication. They stand out, their ideas are seen and heard, and their companies succeed. Decide that being brief is your non-negotiable standard.

As I have seen firsthand, BRIEF tackles an issue that won't go away unless we become lean communicators and let our ideas stand out.

Are you ready?

This won't take long.

[brief]

HOW THE BOOK IS ORGANIZED

PART	INTRO	I	II	III	IV
QUESTION	WHY?	WHY NOW?	HOW?	WHEN/WHERE?	WHAT'S NEXT?
TITLE	Why BRIEF and the New ADD	Heightened Awareness in a World Begging for BRIEF	How to Gain Discipline to be Clear and Concise	Gaining the Decisiveness to Know When and Where to be BRIEF	Being BRIEF: Summary and Action Plan
IN SIX WORDS	Discover BRIEF's main premise and promise	Feed world hunger for the point	Techniques to be clear and concise	Times to deliver "less is more"	Live it daily or lose it
THE GIST	Author's short story behind the birth of BRIEF and what every reader should expect	Flooded with information, interruptions, and inattentive-ness, people are begging for less	Handful of practical approaches to develop the muscle to manage people's attention and stand out	Knowing and navigating the key moments when and where to use lean communication to make an impact	Series of practical insights and challenges to ensure you sustain the skill over time
YOUR FEELING	Curious		Captivated		Committed
BOTTOM LINE	The new, non-negotiable standard in business	A brutal concern and a prerequisite for success today	There's hope for all types of people to tighten up their game	There's a time and place for the "less is more" mandate	Tips to ensure your BRIEF muscle gets in shape and stays that way

HOW TO READ THIS BOOK

BRIEF was deliberately designed to be easy to read and immediately useful. To this end, we've added multiple recurring features and visual elements that quickly grasp the book's benefits.

► **BRIEF BITS** –These short sections offer memorable insights on how to be BRIEF. The military figure accompanying each of them is a reminder that we have to take a more disciplined, mindful approach to be sure we're always clear and concise.

► **BRIEF BASICS**–This handful of critical techniques are essential to being BRIEF. A solid understanding of these BRIEF BASICS is key to being a lean communicator.

► **EXECUTIVE ATTENTION**–Meet two modern executives whose lives are impacted by other people's inability to be BRIEF. Each scene depicts the problems they face and how brevity can turn things around.

Part One
Awareness

Heightened Awareness in a World Begging for BRIEF

1 Why Brevity Is Vital

Long story, short. Executives are busy, and your rambling presentation gets lost in their daily flood of information.

Get to the Point or Pay the Price

You cannot afford to miss the boat on brevity. It's the difference between success and failure. And if you think you've already got it covered, you're wrong.

I've spoken with hundreds of leaders and executives over 20 years and heard countless stories about how someone's inability to get to the point quickly spelled disaster. The dysfunction is real, immediate, and lasting.

Here are a few examples.

- *General dismissal*: A field-grade Army officer uses a series of PowerPoint slides to deliver a brief to his superiors on a recommended strategic course of action. He watches his presentation unravel as a high-ranking general obsessed with details spends the entire time feverishly highlighting every single typographical error on the handout. The officer lost his audience in the minutiae.

- *A rising star stalls*: A brilliant young woman who looks as if she is right out of Central Casting—bright, talented, and attractive—is widely recognized by senior leadership as the future go-to person. Her fatal flaw is well known, however: She cannot close big deals because she cannot shut up. Her motormouth bars her from any client-facing assignments.

- *Done deal comes undone*: After closing a $500,000 contract with a new client, a sales executive is shocked to discover that his overenthusiastic support person has followed up with the client and explained all the reasons why he thinks they've purchased way more technology than they need. The verbal misstep drops the deal by $200,000.

- *98-pager delivered*: A vice president of communications who's frantically looking for a simple, one-page product summary for a big press release discovers that the best her organization can deliver is a mega PowerPoint file with nearly 100 slides. It chokes her e-mail inbox and kills the story.

- *Hero's story overlooked*: A police detective takes the initiative to recognize a fellow officer's generosity and impact with disabled athletes by pitching his feel-good story to a major magazine. A reporter speaks to the detective, who unfortunately cannot quickly sum up his pitch and rambles on. The reporter becomes too confused and doesn't run the story.

- *Luncheon leaves a bad taste*: Three hundred busy executives attend a fundraiser for a nonprofit organization during their busy workweek. The keynote speaker is slotted 20 minutes after the meal. He blows far beyond the allotted time, and after nearly an hour, the room is half empty and the feel-good charity loses its appeal.

You get the point. Today's world is on information overload, and there isn't enough time to sift through all the messages. If you can't capture people's attention and deliver your message with brevity, you'll lose them.

Executive—Interrupted

I once met an executive named Ed who was a lot like many business leaders nowadays—easily distracted.

"I've got way too much going on in my life and in my head," he lamented. "It seems like my mind is under constant assault throughout the day. There are nonstop e-mails, meetings, calls, interruptions, and information," he explained. "It's taxing."

Ed continued, "A few weeks ago. I had a really important meeting with a small agency about the launch of a new advertising campaign targeting younger buyers. It's tough reaching that segment and getting their attention, so I was really interested to see their strategies, timelines, and plans."

Even though Ed disliked meetings, his interest in the topic had him surprisingly geared up. But when I asked how the meeting went, he replied, "We had an hour scheduled. They assured me their PowerPoint was only a few slides, but they were pretty densely packed with research and recommendations. Although they kept the slide count down, they jammed every inch they could."

"They were probably trying to keep it short and to the point for you. But it sounds like there was way too much to cover," I said.

"And that wasn't even half the problem," Ed said. "About 5 minutes into the meeting, I feel my phone go off in my pocket. False alarm—you know, one of those phantom rings when your leg vibrates and the phone's not even there when you check. I eventually found it in my bag—and by then, I'd already been digging around for it and not really paying attention to their presentation."

THE ELUSIVE 600:
MANAGING EXCESS MENTAL BANDWIDTH

People speak about 150 words per minute, yet have the approximate mental capacity to consume about five times that number, or 750 words per minute.

You're having a conversation with some old friends at a college reunion, and they start talking about some hilarious memories. While they're recounting your exploits, your mind immediately **races** to an incident from your senior year with an old flame. You recall in vivid detail how painful it was when you ended the relationship. You imagine the entire break up scene while listening to and laughing with your buddies **at the same time**. Two separate conversations run through your mind simultaneously.

This phenomenon of thinking about one thing while listening to and engaging in a conversation about another is called **the Elusive 600**—and it's always at work. Here's how it happens:

People speak about 150 words per minute, yet they have the approximate mental capacity to consume about five times that number—750 words per minute. So while someone is speaking, you have **600 extra words per minute** to think other thoughts. Your mind's spare bandwidth is always present when you're speaking or listening. This is the cause of many of the issues that make brevity relevant. For example, some implications of the Elusive 600 are:

- ▶ **It can leak.** Others' ideas can easily pop into your mind while you are talking, and you might impulsively start sharing them.

- ▶ **It sets off triggers.** While you are either listening or speaking, a single word or an unrelated distraction can cause you to lose focus.

- ▶ **It needs to be managed.** Whether you're talking or listening, you have the responsibility to manage your Elusive 600.

"Then I notice that I really had gotten a text from my wife, which I of course impulsively check. She tells me that there was a past-due financial aid packet I needed to send in for my daughter's college fall semester—so I have to respond, too."

"It happens to all of us. You've got a smartphone, so people can find you no matter where you are or what you're doing," I add, trying to excuse him.

"Right—but this time I am in a super important meeting, and we are 10 minutes into it and the agency guys start asking me questions. I get a little defensive and even nervous, because I know I haven't been listening carefully," he admits.

"It's like getting caught in high school daydreaming when the teacher calls on you," I sympathize.

"Right. So I try to get things back on track and apologize. I conveniently blame my wife and tell them, 'Let's dive back in.' "I still feel a little disconnected, but I'm committed to focusing on their plan and analysis. Then someone knocks at the door—my coworker, saying that it's really important and will only take a minute. I step out and talk to her about another project that she needs me to make a decision on. It takes 3 or 4 minutes before I cut her short," Ed says.

At this point, it's clear how it all unraveled.

"I return and apologize yet again. Everyone says it's fine, but our momentum slows down more and gives us even less time to discuss. After talking with the team for another few minutes, I start worrying that we are not even close to finishing on time. Handling all the open issues seems like a lost battle, and I start worrying about my next meeting that was right afterward."

"So did you reschedule with the agency?" I asked, wondering if he had realized by that point there was no way to regain their focus or expect them to talk faster.

"No, I just started getting annoyed. I don't know why, but there was a growing tension in the meeting that wasn't there in the beginning."

"But did the agency people help sum up the findings and adjust to the circumstances?"

"No, not really," he says. "They understand how busy I am, but it took them 50 minutes to get to the point. There was too much buildup and no clear message. I know they're brilliant people, but it all got buried."

"Whose fault was it?"

"I am not sure who's to blame, but that tends to keep happening to me. And it's not getting any simpler or clearer. As the day rolls on, the loose ends just build to an overwhelming point," Ed sighs.

"But what if the agency people could have managed *you* better?"

"Me?" Ed looks surprised, and then reconsiders. "Maybe you're right. I was the one checking texts, getting interrupted," he says. "But they should have gotten to the point faster."

"Ed, your world is not getting simpler, and change is not going to stop," I explain in an attempt to make him feel a little better. "The calls, e-mails, texts, social media, and interruptions that require your constant attention are not going away anytime soon."

"The agency—or whoever needs your attention—has to adapt to and manage *you*, and be mindful that this is your life," I say. "The agency's brilliance was lost on you because the presenters failed to find creative ways to cut to the chase and help you get and stay focused."

Who's Responsible for Adapting When the Message Is Not Being Heard?

What happened to Ed happens to executives every day. Who's at fault? Smart people present to busy people, who are constantly flooded with information, are regularly interrupted, are easily distracted, and often grow impatient.

When they don't get the clarity they need quickly, they check out. You've likely been in the same situation when you need to get someone like Ed's attention. You know you have terrific ideas to pitch and important information to share. So how do you get the other person to listen to it?

The modern, multitasking mind is a barrier—and brevity is the key to entry. When you think you have an hour and you wait to deliver the good stuff until the end, you're too late. You already lost your audience—whether it's 1 or 100—in the first few minutes. But if you capture their attention and manage it right away, none of these challenging circumstances will affect your presentation. You have to get to the point in 5 minutes, not 50.

A master of brevity says less and gets more done.

Timing Is of the Essence

It would be a mistake to approach brevity simply from the point of view of time. But a media trainer in New York put it to me this way: "Being brief is not just about time. What's more important is how *long it feels* to the audience."

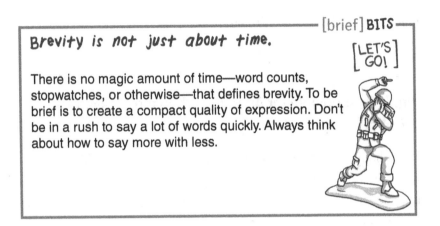

[brief] **BITS**

[LET'S GO!]

Brevity is not just about time.

There is no magic amount of time—word counts, stopwatches, or otherwise—that defines brevity. To be brief is to create a compact quality of expression. Don't be in a rush to say a lot of words quickly. Always think about how to say more with less.

So don't be fooled by a narrow "time is short" view. It's not about using the least amount of time. It's about making the most of the time you have.

BRIEF Balance: The Harmony of Clear, Concise, and Compelling

Not everyone wants people to be brief. Tim McGuire is president of National Merit Scholarship Corporation, the organization that awards $50 million in grants every year to an elite group of about 10,000 high school seniors.

"There's a ton of detail when you're dealing with a brand new group of over 1.5 million individuals every year," McGuire said. "And we have conversations every year with geniuses who were on the cutting room floor because of the limited funding."

The competition is fierce, and every application produces scores of candidates that all look practically the same.

"It's like splitting hairs," he said.

McGuire and National Merit need finalists to expound on their credentials, not trim them, to help break the deadlock.

Cutting out too much detail can actually kill an applicant's chances of getting the scholarship.

Even though potential merit scholars need to divulge lots of details about their achievements, they still need to adhere to the principles of brevity. It's a balancing act of being concise, clear, and compelling. All three need to be in harmony.

Take applicants who need to explain more about their background and extenuating circumstances in one of their final interviews. They need to be clear but cannot let themselves ramble on about a project to oversell their strengths; they still need to be compelling and concise. The interviewer needs to see that the applicants can paint a picture that sets them apart.

To be brief doesn't just mean being concise. Your responsibility is to balance how long it takes to convey a message well enough to cause a person to act on it. That's the harmony of brevity when it's striking the right chords.

A BRIEF Timeout

Let's take a final moment before diving into the book to clarify the kind of brevity we're discussing. There's a tendency to think brevity is pushing for less and runs the risk of being superficial and lacking substance.

Bernie Trilling, Founder and Chief Executive Officer (CEO) of *21st Century Learning Advisors* and coauthor of *21st Century Skills: Learning for Life in Our Times*, coined the terms *light brevity* and *deep brevity* to make this important distinction.

"Light brevity is being concise without comprehension," Trilling said. "Deep brevity is being succinct with savvy."

Brevity starts with deep expertise. Only with thorough knowledge can you accurately make a summary.

"You have to go deep first and be confused for a while," he said. "Then come back up with clarity from a deeper perspective and in that clarity you can be brief."

Being brief can demonstrate how you've gone through that learning experience.

"It's perspective that must come out of deep work," he said. "You've got to give the essence of it. You can't give the whole thing because your audience would have to do the same amount of probing and work."

The road to brevity, then, requires hard work and lots of time. Doing all the digging and analysis on your own time saves the members of your audience from doing the labor themselves.

Timeout is over. Game on.

Long story, short. Executives are busy, and your rambling presentations get lost in their daily flood of information.

2 Mindful of Mind-filled-ness

Long story, short. Today's fast-paced world of information, inattention, interruptions, and impatience requires you to make your point *before* your audience gets distracted.

Brevity Is Like an Instant Stress Release

An executive coach once said to me, "You'd be hard-pressed to find a businessperson say at the end of the day, 'I have some extra mental capacity to handle more.'"

You work around people who are mentally stretched. When you are succinct, you instantly make their life easier. And they remember and are grateful to you for that.

The source of that stress? Executives suffer growing pressure from:

1. *Information inundation*: an unending flood of words, images, sounds, and social media

2. *Inattention*: an inability to stay focused on one item for more than 10 seconds

3. *Interruptions*: a steady stream of problems competing for time and consideration

4. *Impatience*: a growing intolerance for results

This is your world—mine too. And it's only getting worse.

Battling Overcapacity

People can think clearly when they are safe on land. When they are drowning, however, there is only one thing on their mind: finding a life preserver. The new brutal reality is that people are drowning in information. It floods them everywhere they go.

Executives today wake up in the morning and immediately grab their smartphones to check texts, e-mail, updates, sports, stocks, and news. At breakfast, there are tweets and Facebook posts to read and repost. On the commute into the office, they make calls and send and receive a dozen e-mails, all the while trying to "relax" by listening to music.

They get to work to face meeting requests, more e-mails, funny YouTube videos, the company newsletter, and a few voicemails, and then they jump onto the corporate portal. And the day hasn't even started yet.

By the time you step into the picture, their attention is severely taxed. More e-mails, texts, meeting invitations, and pop-up reminders keep them checking their phones nonstop during your meeting.

And although you may get a head nod every once and a while, that doesn't mean you've broken through. They're just being nice.

You need to understand your enemies to defeat them. These four forces are constantly playing against you.

1. Information Inundation—The Water's Rising

"It's like trying to take a drink from a fire hose."

That is how one writer described today's world of information inundation.

An executive explained it to me this way: "I have two meetings per day. They both last an hour. In one group, it takes 50 minutes to get to the point," she said. "I may or may not have the mental stamina to last that long."

The other group gets to the point in the first 10 minutes. The remaining 50 minutes are spent in great conversation about the clarity that was produced in the first few minutes.

"The first group didn't have that sense of clarity and urgency. The second group did and got to the point right up front."

"Maybe they said similar things," she said. "At the end of the day, we really liked the second group and we didn't like the first one."

Software development company Atlassian reported that the average professional receives 304 e-mails per week.[1] According to Kleiner Perkins Caufield & Byers's annual Internet Trends report, people check their phones 150 times per day.[2]

[brief] BITS

Your audience is drowning, and brevity is their lifeline.

[RESCUE MISSION!]

The Elements of Style is a masterpiece guide to good writing—all in less than 100 pages. In it, E. B. White describes Will Strunk's vision, "All through [the book] one finds the author's deep sympathy for the reader. Will felt that the reader was in serious trouble most of the time, a man floundering in a swamp, and that it was the duty of anyone attempting to write to drain this swamp quickly and get this man up on dry ground, or at least throw him a rope."

In a 2012 article in the *International Journal of Communication*, Roger Bohn and James Short of the University of California at San Diego reported that, "in 2008, Americans consumed about 1.3 trillion hours of information outside of work, an average of almost 12 hours per person per day."[3]

304

NUMBER OF E-MAILS AN AVERAGE PROFESSIONAL RECEIVES PER WEEK

150

NUMBER OF TIMES AN AVERAGE PERSON CHECKS THEIR SMARTPHONE PER DAY

28

HOURS EACH WEEK THE AVERAGE PROFESSIONAL SPENDS ON E-MAIL

And the same article reported that the average person consumed 100,500 words on an average day and that workers spent 28 hours a week writing and answering e-mails, searching for information, and collaborating internally.[4]

This pace will only increase. The Radicati Group reported in April 2013 that "the majority of e-mail traffic comes from business e-mails, which accounts for over 100 billion e-mails sent and received per day." Because e-mail is the main way people communicate in business, "This trend is expected to continue, and business e-mail will account for over 132 billion e-mails

85%

PERCENTAGE OF TIME A CEO
SPENDS IN MEETINGS
OR AT PUBLIC EVENTS

sent and received per day by the end of 2017."[5]

Time is even shorter if you are a CEO. The study "What do CEOs do?" revealed that "CEOs spend most of their time (85 percent) with other people. Meetings take up 60 percent of the working hours, and the remaining 25 percent is comprised of phone calls, conference calls, and public events."[6]

We are always connected—in our cars, at home, at work. Everything is a source of information. The implication is that your mastery of brevity—your ability to get to the point *quickly*—will make the difference between being heard or not—and your idea getting through or being dismissed.

2. Inattention—The Muscle Is Weakening

This information inundation is weakening people's ability to focus and prioritize. Prevailing research says that the average attention span is down to 8 seconds from 12 over the past five years.[7]

Being interrupted many times over a long period of time wears down your mental capacity, according to author David Rock. In his book *Your Brain at Work*, Rock writes, "Change focus 10 times an hour (one study showed people in offices did so as much as 20 times an hour), and your productive thinking time is only a fraction of what's possible. Less energy equals less capacity to understand, decide, recall, memorize, and inhibit. The result could be mistakes on important tasks."[8]

Busy professionals constantly face demands on their time and attention. They can't handle any more.

Executives from all levels constantly tell me they are exhausted by the end of the workday and feel as if they have attention-deficit disorder (ADD). Their attention spans seem jumpy and unfocused. In fact, some scientists believe that people who are "always on" and taking in information actually experience temporarily lowered IQs—and can experience a temporary drop of up to 10 IQ points.[9]

In addition, a group of Stanford University researchers studied frequent multitaskers and found that they have a more difficult time paying attention to the various forms of media they are exposed to than those who only occasionally multitask.[10] "When they're in situations where there are multiple sources of information coming from the external world or emerging out of memory, they're not able to filter out what's not relevant to their current goal," said associate professor and study author Anthony Wagner. "That failure to filter means they're slowed down by that irrelevant information."[11]

Think of attention span as a muscle. It begins to tire if we use it all day long in lots of different ways. People's attention is much stronger in the morning than in the afternoon. And if we treat all information equally, it increasingly affects our ability to hold our attention for a certain period of time.

3. Interruption—The Rate Is Alarming

Researchers say the average worker experiences one interruption every 8 minutes, or six to seven interruptions per hour. That equals 50 to 60 interruptions in an 8-hour day.

We're also interrupting ourselves. You've likely been working on a difficult task when something easier or more engaging competes for your attention. Naturally, we feel like doing *that* instead. It's almost Pavlovian.

60
NUMBER OF TIMES A
WORKER IS INTERRUPTED
EACH DAY—ONCE EVERY
8 MINUTES

25
NUMBER OF MINUTES
IT TAKES TO RETURN TO A
TASK AFTER YOU'VE BEEN
INTERRUPTED

$588B
AMOUNT THAT
INTERRUPTIONS COST
BUSINESSES EACH YEAR

For example, imagine I'm working in a quiet room on an important project, reading, writing, and developing deeper insights and analyses. Soon I'm thinking: "This is starting to get really hard. It'd be easier to check my phone." So I stop doing what I am doing.

Or maybe I am reading a colleague's e-mail that's a little too long and tough to follow. It's hard to concentrate, because the writer is not getting to the point. So I decide to put it aside for something less taxing, and I check the other messages or text someone.

Gloria Mark, a professor of informatics at the University of California, Irvine, found that the average worker spent 11 minutes and 4 seconds on a task before being interrupted or interrupting himself or herself and switching to another task. Mark explains that once interrupted, it takes an average of 25 minutes for a worker to return to the original task.[12]

In fact, an average worker loses 2.1 hours per day to "unimportant interruptions and distractions," according to a study by Basex. Interruptions come at a high cost to businesses—specifically, to the tune of $588 billion a year in lost revenue.[13]

E-mail is a big interrupter. A study in the *International Journal of Human-Computer Interaction* by Karen Renaud, Judith Ramsay, and Mario Hair report that "office workers who use computers ... constantly stop what they're doing to read and respond to incoming emails. It's not unusual for them to glance at their inbox 30–40 times an hour (though when asked how frequently they look, they'll give a much lower figure)."[14]

4. Impatience—The Ice Is Thinning

The conditions of today's workflow have prompted people to expect things to happen faster. For instance, if you're reading a magazine on a tablet, the typical way to change a page is to flick your finger. It's so easy. People are carrying volumes of information on a thin tablet and can navigate this information by barely lifting a finger.

When I want to read the *Wall Street Journal*, I just download it. I don't have to walk out of my house to get it. It downloads within seconds, and I am reading it on my couch with a cup of coffee made instantly by a Keurig machine. Yet I get easily frustrated if the page doesn't load fast enough.

We don't spend much time on any *one* task. What's the average time an American spends looking at a Web page? 56 seconds. How about watching a YouTube video? In 2010, it took only 3.95 minutes.[15]

Technology has created an unwritten expectation that things will just go faster. So if you fail to make your point with people as quickly as they'd like, they might lose patience.

This contributes to our impatience with everyday events like meetings—a place where executives spend much of their time. In the book *Meeting by Design*, author Michael Clargo reports that, "almost 50 percent of meetings fail to use people's time efficiently … we have twice as many meetings and they last twice as long as would be necessary if they were properly designed and run."[16]

Google's approach to this problem is to project the image of a 4-foot stopwatch on the wall that counts down the meeting's time so it cannot run over.[17] The sheer size of the clock reminds attendees just how precious each minute is. Time cannot slip through your fingers when the minute hand is as long as your arm.

What Does It All Mean?

If you're adding more information, interruption, time, or complexity to others' day, all you're doing is encouraging them to tune you out. And if you don't develop a heightened awareness of this issue, you're training people to block you out permanently.

These days, it's no longer possible to get by on the merit of your idea, title, or allotted time. You have to put it in a smaller package and make it easier to consume and digest. You must boil it down and get to the point quickly, or be forgotten.

Your New Reality: There's No Time for a Slow Buildup

That is the reality today. There's no time to build up to a big conclusion. To communicate effectively nowadays, you must be able to speak in headlines and grab someone's attention right away.

Take, for example, a senior vice president of corporate communications who was managing significant organizational changes. He had two CEOs inside of one year, an activist board of directors, and public issues of tremendous significance.

The nature of the senior VP's job was clearly changing, and he needed to adapt. The board of directors—as well as industry and community leaders—were putting him under much more scrutiny and quickly growing impatient.

It was obvious in my conversations with him that the issue of strategic communications was on the front lines. More than ever in his career, he was running out of time and needed to create clarity, urgency, and context for people who didn't care to wade through mounds of detail. His key stakeholders all had questions and needed answers quickly.

Board members were very busy and had little patience. Their attention was divided between the issues of the senior VP's company and those of other companies they ran or advised. He explained that their knowledge was a mile wide and an inch deep.

"Anytime my staff tries to present to them, the board members are checking their smartphones during meetings, excusing themselves to take phone calls, or just looking at them with eyes glazed over," he complained. "I realized that my staff needed to hit the ground running and interact with them in a more succinct way, or our company would be seriously affected."

He continued, "As activist investors, they weren't interested in the slow build. We need to find a way to overcome their inattention, interruptions, and impatience—to communicate to them in a quick and concise way. It's our new standard and our new reality."

"How are you adapting," I asked, "considering this new standard of brevity comes with the realization that there is no longer the time or attention that we used to have?"

"My new world doesn't have time like it used to. We have to get to the point faster—because these key people will make decisions for us if we don't do it," he said.

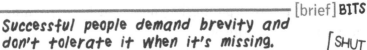

Successful people demand brevity and don't tolerate it when it's missing.

Busy people quickly lose patience when their peers and subordinates cannot get to the point. If you're buried under hundreds of e-mails and are in meetings all day, you don't have the time to waste on people droning on.

In their world—and likely yours as well—brevity is the new unspoken expectation.

Test Yourself

Where can you begin to get through to your audience more effectively?

Following are a few questions you can use to assess your mastery of this critical skill. Take a moment to think about how well you and your organization do some or all of the following things:

Examination of Brevity

1. Can I hear an hour's worth of complex information and summarize it in a 2-minute debrief?

2. Do I write e-mails that get to the point in five lines or less?

3. Do my PowerPoint presentations contain fewer than 10 slides, with plenty of images and little text?

4. Can I translate complicated ideas into a simple story, analogy, or anecdote?

5. Can I expertly deliver headlines like a reporter?

6. Do I speak clearly and concisely—in plain English rather than confusing corporate speech or jargon?

7. Do I know instantly when I've "lost" somebody?

In the coming chapters, we will examine how to master these skills and when to use them.

A New Professional Standard

Get ready—it's a whole new world. If you are used to preparing a seven-course meal, get ready to serve tapas. You and your company are going to stand out and get people's attention. You are going to be remembered and your ideas are going to be sticky. Everyone else will get left behind. Now is the time to turn the negative force of our attention economy on its head. Lean communication is your new advantage.

Long story, short. Today's fast-paced world of information, inattention, interruptions, and impatience requires you to make your point *before* your audience gets distracted.

3 Why You Struggle with Brevity: The Seven Capital Sins

Long story, short. Brevity is difficult to master because there are many subtle, unconscious "seven capital sins" that can interfere.

Why Is It So Difficult?

Why can't we simply add "being succinct" to our tool belt, alongside punctuality and neat handwriting? There is no single reason why people find it hard to be brief. Love of talking seems to be the logical front-runner, but in reality, it is among a short list of seven key contributors that can be deadly if left unchecked.

Which ones do you struggle with? Be honest—chances are that more than one applies to you.

1. *Cowardice*: "I am afraid that it's hard to say. There are a lot of perspectives on that topic." Please take a stand and tell us what you really think.

2. *Confidence*: "I know the material so well I could talk about it for days." Save us the time, and don't.

3. *Callousness*: "This will only take a minute ... " Really? Do you not see how busy I am? When you don't respect people's time, it always turns into an hour.

4. *Comfort*: "Once I start talking, it feels so soothing and I just get on a roll." Can you have the discipline to hit the Stop button?

5. *Confusion*: "Bear with me; I am just thinking out loud." Well, your mind is a mess—why do you have to share it with us?

6. *Complication*: "That is a really intricate issue. You cannot explain it easily." But your job is to simplify it for us.

7. *Carelessness*: "Did I say that out loud?" Um, yes you did, so use a filter next time.

It is not enough to simply *understand* the need for brevity. You need to go deeper and figure out why it's so difficult for you to get to the point. Brevity is a habit, and this short list of vices must be addressed to develop it. So compare your situation with those shown in the illustrations for each sin, and be honest—which ones do you need to confess?

1. Cowardice

- *Issue*: You hide behind meaningless words and don't have the guts to be clear and take a stand. You're afraid someone will challenge or disagree with you, so you mask your message in mounds of jargon and buzzwords and always take the middle road.

- *Illustration*: You work for a global manufacturing company and specialize in supply chain logistics. It is a complex business with plenty of nuance, change, and pressures. When you speak, you crank out waves of PowerPoint slides and rattle out business-speak that leaves management wondering, "What did you just say?"

- *Impact*: Your leadership team doesn't know what to do with your assessment and guidance and subconsciously starts questioning your leadership ability. "What is your recommendation or plan of attack?" they wonder. When someone who is braver and clearer steps up, you're history.

2. Confidence

- *Issue*: You are a know-it-all and, to everyone's dismay, cannot restrain yourself from explaining every painful detail. The word *pedantic* suits you perfectly, and you believe you could teach a class on your favorite topic.

- *Illustration*: You are a subject matter expert on Internet security. You write books, white papers, and blogs on the topic, and you are frequently invited to give speeches on the matter. One would expect your talks to be interesting, but they're long, dry, and technical. Even your stories are boring, and your e-mails read like a dissertation.

- *Impact*: Nobody likes to talk to you because once you start, there is little they can do to stop you. You are a smart person, but you don't see your own weakness. People ignore or instantly delete your e-mails. Over the course of your career, your specialty knowledge and knack for being long-winded impede your career growth.

3. Callousness

- *Issue*: You are selfish and don't respect people's time. Even though you are in a hurry when people speak to you, time stands still when you have the floor. When you ask, "Got a minute?" you really mean, "I will stay as long as possible."

- *Illustration*: You approach Victor (who's on a deadline) at his desk. You need to ask him an important question for a project you are working on. You peek in, make quick eye contact, and interrupt him. He stops what he's doing, and you start talking. You have no clue that every word you say is making him late. He thinks, "You don't care about anyone but yourself." And he's fuming inside.

- *Impact*: If people see that you don't respect their time, they'll stop respecting you. During your review, you get low scores from your peers.

[brief] **BITS**

It's time to stop talking when you start enjoying what you're saying.

According to media expert Dan Broden, one of the best times to stop talking in an interview is when you've given a clear answer that you're passionate about and would love to discuss more. Have the discipline to stop, let the reporter catch what you're saying, and invite you to build on it. Call it a permission pause.

---

4. Comfort

- *Issue*: You let yourself get loose and wordy with people who know you. Familiarity breeds contempt and lack of brevity. You have a double standard: you're succinct with important people, yet long-winded with those you know well.

- *Illustration*: It is late Friday afternoon, and you run into your boss coming back from a meeting. He asks you casually if you have weekend plans, and you have plenty. About midway through your 15-minute verbal tour, your boss starts to wonder, "Maybe I should not have asked—and taken a differ-ent route back from my meeting."

- *Impact*: There's a time and place for small talk. You must always be aware that what is exciting for you to share could be agony for someone else. You should treat everyone the same way; they are busy and begging you to be brief.

5. Confusion

- *Issue*: You choose to think out loud when it is still not clear to you what you are thinking—which is a big mistake. When ideas are still germinating, they will likely be out of order, indistinct, and blurry. And that's okay, as long as you don't trot them out in public.

- *Illustration*: You are a senior director at an engineering firm and love to brainstorm new ideas. Not all of them are spot on, but you love the creative process and cannot contain your enthusiasm when describing what might be the next big break-through. Those around you often sit in silence listening to your brain run wild and meander through the verbal trees.

- *Impact*: Even though your idea is still developing and in lots of pieces, people will make judgments about you and your abilities. You should choose carefully when and where—and to whom—you think out loud.

6. Complication

- *Issue*: You firmly believe that there are some things too com-plex to be simplified—even though the world highly values people who can simplify difficult concepts.

- *Illustration*: You get a phone call from a client asking about a delivery on a late order. Aware of all the background issues that are plaguing the project, you decide to give a lengthy answer to justify the unexpected delays. The client not only is unhappy but also is now worried that there might be quality issues if manufacturing is as complicated as the customer service rep's explanations.

- *Impact*: When people want a simple answer, you need to give it to them. When they don't get it, they lose patience and trust.

7. Carelessness

- *Issue*: You are often verbally sloppy and let your mind and message get mixed up, leaving people guessing and frustrated.

- *Illustration*: You have just seen a key client and want to debrief your boss on the status of a new contract, so you call him late one night. You weren't expecting voicemail, but decide anyway to leave a message that is all over the board. You know it wasn't the best, but you think you can clean up the mess tomorrow. You even send an e-mail to your boss (that is not much better). Your boss checks voicemail and e-mail later that night and loses confidence in your ability to communicate well with clients.

- *Impact*: Being mentally and verbally lazy sends a clear message: you might not be ready for the next assignment—or even be the right person for the job.

You need to hold yourself to a higher standard when you are dealing with people professionally: Do you get to the point?

It is your responsibility to change, so don't expect others to put up with your seven capital sins. Consider this list to be a personal checklist of what you need to work on to become a lean communicator and a master of brevity. In all of these areas, there are opportunities for you to make an immediate change that translates into greater results for a variety of professional circumstances.

Long story, short. Brevity is difficult to master because there are many subtle, unconscious "seven capital sins" that can interfere.

4 The Big Bang of Brevity

Long story, short. Be disciplined, respectful, and well prepared, and your clients will thank you.

A Success Story

Not every executive has a bad experience when it comes to brevity. There are success stories that make an immediate impact during the course of busy people's schedules. Here's one.

I once worked with a finance executive named Edna, who told me about a positive experience she had with one of her consulting firms. She is a senior executive who operates at a fast pace and processes a ton of information every day—checking e-mails and answering phone calls and questions from her staff. She's in high demand because she has a tremendous capacity to process and make quick decisions.

But like a lot of people, Edna can be easily distracted and inattentive. She has a short fuse and is very driven to get things done. To win with her, you have to capture her imagination and get to the point. She's the face of today's executive.

TRIMMING:
LEVEL 1 TO 3 DETAILS

Cut out unnecessary details from your story.

An exercise I use to test workshop participants' ability to edit out unnecessary information is to ask them to think of a defining professional moment. I give them about 10 to15 minutes to prepare for a 3-minute presentation. Many of them get visibly excited when they decide what to share.

Then I tell them to present to a partner who listens, takes notes, and shares a **1-minute** version to the rest of the group.

When telling a story, Level 1 details are those that are absolutely **essential;** Level 2 points are those that add a little flavor but not too much more time; and Level 3 items weigh it down and don't make the story noticeably better.

This challenge forces them to start **trimming.** To hit the 1-minute mark means only Level 1 and a few Level 2 details.

Implications:

► **Ensure instant appreciation.** People are thankful when it requires less energy to grasp the same basic information in less time.

► **Live the "less is more" way.** When you are throwing things out, it may be hard to decide what goes—but keep in mind what people will really care about.

► **Look for what weighs you down.** Cutting out the finer detail requires attention and awareness for what unnecessarily burdens people.

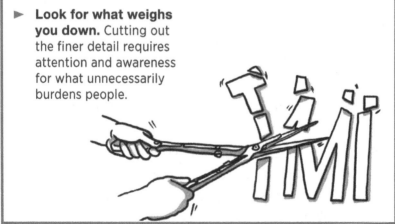

"The meetings that I have typically feel the same way. We sit down, there are introductions, a PowerPoint presentation, my texts start to come and the interruptions begin, people check their phones during the meeting, I check my e-mail, people zone in and out," she said.

"However, I was surprised one day when my consulting company came in and was happy to find that they've adapted to this new reality. The first thing they did was give me a very powerful and very clear executive summary—all of their findings right up front, with no 'slow build.'

"They gave us the headline right out of the gate: 'This is what we've found, and this is what we think you should do,'" Edna explained. "All of that happened within the first 5 or 10 minutes of the meeting. Even though I gave them an hour, they assumed they had to be done with all of the substantive conclusions and insights in the first few minutes. They really framed the headline right up front," she said.

By serving the meat of their presentation first, the client ensured that Edna wasn't lost when the initial interruption came with a knock at the door. "I already had a clear indication of the direction of the meeting before people started hovering outside my door," she said. "I felt like I had what I needed."

This sense of being concise carried over to the rest of Edna's meeting. "Their PowerPoint presentation was much thinner, with only a dozen slides. They were not speaking to the slides, but *with* me," Edna explained. "Every one had a strong headline and a strong visual."

"What was the atmosphere like in the room?" I asked.

"Everybody was engaged in conversation. The consultants were talking *with* me, not presenting *at* me. They stopped talking and let me talk, which was really great for me. I felt like they wanted to have a discussion and listen more."

Annoyed to distraction

► Your rambling presentation gets lost in their daily flood of information. Stop them from drowning.

"Did you get interrupted?"

"Yes, but when distractions came, I wasn't even tempted to acknowledge them because I was so engrossed in the conversation we were having. I ignored the people at the door."

The consultants also used lots of strong visuals, including a short video clip that illustrated a case study. According to Edna, "We talked for about 45 minutes, and they got to the point so quickly that they finished early."

And this is their regular MO. "That's just the way they operate," Edna explained. "In every engagement, they are prepared to have an executive summary conversation with me as opposed to an hour-long presentation. I love talking to them."

Edna also added their communication approach carries over to other interactions with the company: their calls are short, they are prepared, and they anticipate and invite her questions and give her time to process. And their e-mails are always tight.

"I actually look forward to meeting with them. It tends to be the highlight of my day, because they know how to get my attention," Edna said. "Everybody on their team is like that. It's a breath of fresh air."

Long story, short. Be disciplined, respectful, and well prepared, and your clients will thank you.

[brief] BITS

[GIVE IT TO ME STRAIGHT!]

Conversations always beat presentations.

Kenneth Blanchard, author of *The One Minute Manager*, said, "I saw a guy give a motivational speech recently. He had seven secrets to success, and it took him 45 minutes to do the first four. You could see the audience squirming in their seats. They were, like, 'Oh God, there are three more?'" Talk *with* them, not at them. Give them a way to interact and participate.

Part Two
Discipline
How to Gain Discipline to Be Clear and Concise

5 Mental Muscle Memory to Master Brevity

Long story, short. It's not enough to know *why* you need to say less. There are four proven techniques that will ensure you gain this powerful muscle.

The Exercise of Brevity

Tackling a topic like brevity is ambitious. Early on in the project, friends and family would ask me, "How's the book going?" The question was innocent enough but tough to answer *briefly*. So I decided I needed a metaphor.

"It's like cutting down a huge tree, like a redwood. You can show up with an ax, but it's not enough," I'd explain. "You have to think about *how* you're going to do it."

A book about brevity cannot just touch on *why* it's needed. You need a plan of attack—details on *how* you're going to change. Over the years, I've seen people in a variety of professions experience aha moments of brevity. I've helped busy executives, intense Army officers, cynical sales directors, and many others grapple with this daunting challenge.

In Part Two, I will teach *you* how to master this skill.

I've based it on four proven approaches. You can use each of them alone or together to create *mental muscle memory*, that is, habits we should adopt and never abandon because they make us better professionals.

The approach looks something like this:

- *Map it.* BRIEF Maps are used to condense and trim volumes of information.

- *Tell it.* Narrative storytelling is used to explain in a way that's clear, concise, and compelling.

- *Talk it.* TALC Tracks turn monologues into controlled conversations.

- *Show it.* Visuals attract attention and capture imagination.

Each of these helps you manage people's mind-filled-ness and keeps them focused and on track.

Long story, short. It is not enough to know *why* you need to say less. There are four proven techniques that will ensure you gain this powerful muscle.

6 Map It: From Mind Mapping to BRIEF Maps

L **ong story, short.** Professionals mistakenly abandon outlines, but a BRIEF Map is a new visual outlining tool that prepares you to be succinct.

Your 11th Grade English Teacher Was Right

Working from an outline is always a good idea. As the father in a large family, I get lots of opportunities to edit my kids' school papers. And even though it can be painful at times, I encourage them to use me as a sounding board. As a matter of principle, I always ask them for an outline.

"Guys, I'm in the word business," I tell them. "I can help edit your papers, but you're going to need to give me an outline first."

One of my daughters, Isabel, was tackling a particularly tough high school term paper on freedom of speech. It was an important project for her junior year coursework. She had been working on it for months, and it needed to be eight pages long.

"Dad, I have so much research; I don't know where to start," Isabel complained as the deadline quickly approached.

"Don't worry; just show me your outline," I said, knowing that her teacher expected one, too.

"Oh, I've got one done already."

"Okay, I'd love to see it," I replied. But it never appeared. Instead, she quickly planted the rough draft in front of me before I could stop her.

"Just look at the first few pages. I need to know if I'm on the right track," Isabel said. I dove in and started editing. Before I knew it, I was hacking her paper to pieces with a red pen. She started getting defensive. It was not an enjoyable experience for either of us.

We would have averted much of the confusion and tension if Isabel had completed an outline. Outlines organize and prioritize thoughts with clarity and logic, and help stop nonsensical rambling.

Yet professionals seem to think they can outgrow outlines. Although it's a common requirement in school, people abandon them as they get older. This is especially true—surprisingly—when preparing for important communication, whether it's a big pitch, meeting, progress report, or e-mail correspondence. There's no outline to be seen.

It's a huge mistake to make, especially when you consider the vast amount of information you have to handle, distill, and disseminate in these situations.

So let's go back to Isabel for a moment. Assume that most of her classmates did the same thing she did: completed a half-hearted outline or none at all. Then consider how hard it was for her teacher to read all of their semicoherent papers.

I did some quick calculations: There were about 100 students submitting the paper, or about 800 pages to correct. If each one took 5 minutes, the teacher had more than 60 hours of correcting to do.

In this instance, Isabel's teacher did this tedious work of editing over her spring break. Ouch—clearly no vacation.

Now imagine if that poor teacher were your client.

How many hours of half-prepared, semiorganized conversations, meetings, and e-mails have you had without preparing a basic outline? Imagine the confusion and mental agony you've caused over the years by having an "I'll just wing it" attitude in the following situations—among others.

EXCUSE-TO-IMPACT RATIO

EXCUSE	IMPACT
I'm in a hurry; It's just a meeting.	No guarantee of support
I'm running into a meeting.	No clear direction
I'll just fire off a quick e-mail.	No response; e-mail deleted
I'm in a meeting, I'll just use my slides.	No clear understanding of material
I've got a conference; I'll see who I meet.	No strong impression made
I'm giving a sales pitch.	No request for proposal
I'm making a follow- up call.	No new project opportunity
I'm going into an interview.	No job offer

An Outline Is Missing, and So Is the Sale

Let's explore how a sales pitch can go south in the absence of outlining. Landon is a senior sales rep who never uses outlines to prepare for presentations or to follow up with important accounts. He prepares, but just in his mind—never in writing. He excuses himself from planning in advance using one reason or another (not enough time, he's done this presentation countless times before, etc.). And disaster ensues.

When Landon speaks, he lacks discipline. His PowerPoints run over an hour every time, his follow-up e-mails go for paragraphs, his account plans for his boss are at least 20 pages each and rife with unnecessary details, and even his social media status updates include pointless blurbs about what he had for breakfast. Worst of all, his sales pitch is not only too long but also filled with disconnected thoughts and excessive details.

If Landon had the habit of outlining, his colleagues and clients would notice.

The people you deal with every day are on the receiving end of overexplained, underprepared, and complicated communication. They suffer in the same way as Landon's prospective clients, who silently think, "So what's the point?" They wonder why they don't get what he's saying, and he ends up suffering in weaker sales, confused customers, and harsh performance reviews.

This happens to you as well. But you can avoid it if you start by sketching out your ideas in an *outline*.

Five immediate benefits to outlining are they keep you:

- *Prepared*: I'm ready to deliver.
- *Organized*: I understand how all my ideas connect.
- *Clear*: I'm certain what my point is.
- *Contextual*: I can draw a bigger picture so my point stands out.
- *Confident*: I know what to say, inside and out.

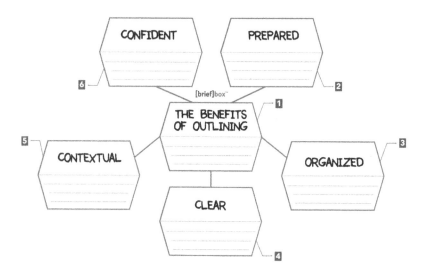

Outlines are worth the effort. The potential pain it takes to create one is a small sacrifice for the confusion you avoid and the time you save.

Mind Mapping and the Modern Outline

Despite a growing aversion to traditional outlines, the practice of mind mapping—or visual outlining—is spreading steadily through the business world.

Its adoption makes sense, since all the ingredients that make this method so attractive are present nowadays: a widespread adoption of software, broad use of whiteboards, growing impatience with linear learning, and a strong preference for visual presentations.

Chuck Frey, an evangelist and expert on the art of mind mapping, discusses the obvious value of these visual outlines[1]:

Mind mapping software is particularly well suited to information triage, because it enables you to gather, organize, evaluate, and take action on a vast amount of information, knowledge, and ideas ... by giving you the power to move topics and subtopics around, attach notes, links, and documents to them that provide meaning and context, and play "what if" with your ideas. No other type of software provides the power and flexibility offered by mind mapping software for manipulating information and ideas.

Mind maps are spreading organically via word of mouth through evangelical adopters like Frey. He explains that companies such as Boeing embrace them enthusiastically because "they provide a skeletal view that lets you think about your thinking."

Mind maps are gaining ground as commonplace work tools; Boeing even has an internal forum to promote and support them.

Mind mapping software providers like Mindjet—the current category leader that has more than 80 percent of the Fortune 100 using its product—are giving individuals a simpler and more powerful tool to wrestle with information overload and put order to chaos.[2]

[brief] BITS

It takes time to be ready to say less.

[GET READY!]

Most people are too busy—or lazy—to take the time to prepare to be brief. Blaise Pascal said, "I have only made this letter longer because I have not had the time to make it shorter." If you don't make the effort and take the time, there will be confusion. Horace warned, "Brevis esse laboro, obscurus fio." ("When I try to be brief, I become unclear.")

What makes software like Mindjet—and even free, toned-down tools like Bubbl.us—so appealing is that they're highly visual, logical, and intuitive to use and share.

BRIEF Maps: A Practical Tool for Delivering Brevity

The growing number of companies embracing mind maps led me to see what all the fuss was about. So I decided to develop a specific type of mind map—a BRIEF Map—to improve communication by simplifying complex messages into a one-page visual outline.

BRIEF maps explain and summarize important information. They're highly useful and practical for executive teams to use. Maps can outline progress reports, capture meeting summaries, and synthesize strategies. They can articulate a corporate vision, isolate a key aspect of a new product, or simplify a complex initiative or issue that could potentially take a long time to understand.

Maps keep the topic on track—and keep it clear and consistent.

Each of the letters in the word *BRIEF* stands for a specific function of one of the bubbles on the map. The middle bubble, which is the focal point or headline of your communication, is called the Brief Box. Before building a BRIEF Map, I recommend using a worksheet (see the following diagram) that captures everything you might say and determining its order and logic. After you have this in place, it's time to draw it out.

Every BRIEF Map is organized in the following way:

B: Background or beginning

R: Reason or relevance

I: Information for inclusion

E: Ending or conclusion

F: Follow-up or questions you expect to be asked or that you might ask

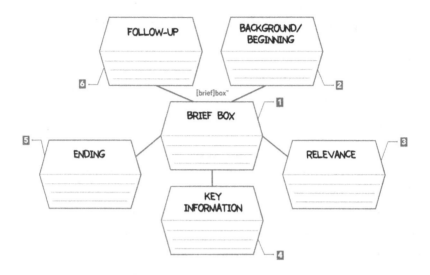

How a BRIEF Map Can Be Used

Consider the following scenario: Bob is working on a project to replace some crucial technology and update his company's IT infrastructure in such a way that will ensure rapid growth. He must provide regular reports on the process to the CEO. They are about halfway done, and the president, who is aware of the project's strategic importance, needs an update from Bob.

Wrong Approach: Bob Chooses to Share but Not to Prepare

The project has had more than its share of frustrations, including unclear expectations, cost overruns, and delays. Despite these challenges, it's an important chance for Bob to prove his talent and possibly get a promotion. There's a lot on the line for both him and his company. He understandably wants to make a positive impression on the president, so he decides to stop by his office to give a quick update.

Bob starts out well by hitting on some key highlights. However, he starts to stray a bit, and it's unclear how this update addresses some of the pressing issues. The CEO gets lost in too many minuscule details; when he starts drilling down, Bob becomes flustered and defensive. The conversation goes long and it ends inconclusively. The CEO is beginning to wonder if the project will succeed—and both he and Bob are beginning to lose confidence.

Right Approach: Bob Prepares a BRIEF Map and Maintains Executive Support

Bob recognizes before the meeting that the president doesn't have a lot of time, so he draws up this BRIEF Map to keep his context airtight and to the point.

Step 1: The BRIEF Box

♦ Bob crafts a strong headline—his BRIEF Box—that reads "The project is on schedule."

Step 2: B, or the Background/Beginning

♦ Bob thinks, "Okay—how am I going to start the update after the headline? What's my beginning or background statement? Well, the last time I talked with the CEO, he had a series of questions and needed me to look into some issues. Since that's what we last spoke about and what he remembers, I should start there. That's how I'll warm things up the first few minutes and explain why I'm coming in today." And so Bob begins by saying, "I've got an update to the last question you asked."

Step 3: R, or Reason/Relevance

♦ Bob thinks, "What's the reason I'm talking to him *now?* Why is it urgent and relevant to do so at this time?" Bob makes a clear connection to the last few updates and states his headline up front, while explaining that he needs to procure a few additional items to keep the project on track.

Step 4: I, or Key Information

♦ Bob thinks, "What will the core of the update include?" He determines three key elements that he would like to share—his select details and bullet points:

Where has there been progress?
Is the project still on schedule?
What specifically is needed?
With these three points lined up, ready, and in order, Bob's made it easy for the CEO to change gears mentally and track the progress report.

Step 5: E, or Intended Ending

♦ There needs to be an intended moment when the update will end and Bob can confidently conclude. Bob has outlined a few next steps that will be followed, and he concludes by saying, "I will get you a price summary and the new timeline tomorrow."

Step 6: F, or Expected Follow-up Questions

♦ Finally, Bob stops to carefully consider any and all questions he thinks the CEO might ask. This gives even more insight he can use to make his BRIEF Map clearer and tighter. He thinks, "If I give him the update that we're making progress with the technology and are on schedule, I want him to give me feedback and ask some questions. That will be how I know it went well and whether it was clear."

♦ He correctly anticipates that the boss might have questions such as: Is this going to cost us any downtime or put us over budget? Are there any unseen risks? Sure enough, when Bob brings those up, the CEO thinks Bob's reading his mind.

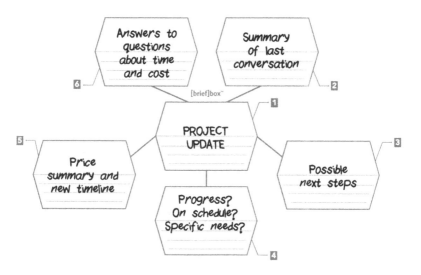

Result: A Successful Update

Because Bob prepared all this in his BRIEF Map, he was able to provide a very clear, consistent, and well-prepared update that was easy for the CEO to follow. Bob walked in *prepared* and delivered his update in less than 5 minutes. The CEO was satisfied and gave Bob the support and endorsement he was seeking. All because Bob took the extra time *to prepare to be brief.*

As one executive famously said, "Be brief and be gone."

▶ As the day wears on, their attention becomes exhausted and unfocused. Do the work for them.

BRIEF Maps: What's the Payoff?

Brevity is all about preparation and preassembly. When you successfully prepare to deliver these important messages, you are confident that you've already thought through the key information your audience needs. You're giving people a preconstructed message.

Imagine it is Christmas Eve. You bought your child a bicycle, but you realize, "Oh no, I have to assemble it." Now imagine the relief you feel as you look at the box and see the words "No assembly required."

A BRIEF Map does the same thing: you give a person a "no assembly required" message. That person feels that same sense of relief you did when you saw those words on the bicycle's box—and will reap the same benefits.

There are no loose parts lying around. The bike is ready to ride.

Long story, short. Professionals mistakenly abandon outlines, but a BRIEF Map is a new visual outlining tool that prepares you to be succinct.

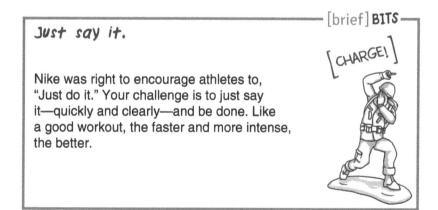

[brief] BITS

Just say it.

[CHARGE!]

Nike was right to encourage athletes to, "Just do it." Your challenge is to just say it—quickly and clearly—and be done. Like a good workout, the faster and more intense, the better.

7 Tell It: The Role of Narratives

Long story, short. People are buried in corporate-speak, but you can help them by embracing narrative storytelling to be clear, concise, and compelling.

I'm Tired of Meaningless and Meandering Corporate Jargon. I'm Ready for a Good Story.

"Every once in a while, a revolutionary product comes along that changes everything," so said Steve Jobs at the start of his legendary presentation unveiling the first iPhone at MacWorld in 2007.[1]

This presentation, which you can watch on YouTube, is a terrific example of how businesses can use narratives to deliver key messages. He might not have been aware of it, but Jobs was building a strategic narrative to make his keynote presentation tight.

First, *he stated his purpose* for being on stage that day: "Today, Apple is going to reinvent the phone."

Jobs then talked about how Apple was a company that was always introducing these breakthrough products that really served a fundamental need people had—from the Macintosh to the iPod and iTunes.

All good narratives *have a villain or a conflict.* In this story, it was Apple's competitors, Jobs explained, who were not doing their job. Their mobile phones were hard to use and not very intuitive.

"The most advanced phones are called smartphones. They say it's the Internet. It's sort of the baby Internet," he said, mocking his rivals. "They are not so smart and they are not so easy to use."

Jobs argued that Apple needed to step up and create a breakthrough device that not only would be smart and easy to use but also would solve a lot of problems that users encountered with many mobile devices. People needed to be able to browse the Internet, make phone calls, and listen to music on a user-friendly device. He *explained his brand's intentions*: "What we want to do is make a leapfrog product that is way smarter than any mobile device has ever been, and super-easy to use."

He *strengthened the core presentation* by explaining how Apple was going to deliver on his bold promise to improve the user interface and phone software: "Who wants a stylus? You have to get them and put them away, and you lose them. Yuck. Nobody wants a stylus .... [the iPhone is] far more accurate than any touch display that has ever been shipped. It ignores unintended touches; it's super-smart. You can do multifinger gestures on it."

At the end, there was an explosive round of applause from an audience that understood the full impact of why iPhone would be one of the most revolutionary and pervasive devices.

Instead of launching into a list of all the phone's features, Jobs first chose to tell the members of his audience a *compelling story* they would all embrace. It's a wonderful example of how a product launch can be fundamentally different if it's *framed in a narrative.* The personal connection was immediate and lasting.

━[brief] BASICS━

TELLING VS. SELLING:
STORYTELLING TRUMPS PERSUATION

Telling your audience a well-researched and well-structured story is more effective than just selling your point of view.

While I was a senior vice president at marketing and PR agency Ketchum, I participated in many presentations to land new accounts, such as Visa, IBM, and Kodak. After leaving, one of my new clients asked me to sit on the other side of the table to help them select a PR agency. I was thrilled to see what the process looked like from the client's perspective.

We sat through six new business presentations that lasted an hour each. My impression was that **they all sounded basically the same,** except one: a firm called Edelman. Their team, led by Randy Pitzer, stood out because they did their homework and **told the client** in full detail how their market was changing. They immersed themselves in the narrative and had a **conversation** that positioned the client at the center of the story and gave them a way to emerge victorious. It was clear, plausible, and strategic.

After the pitch day was over, the head of corporate communications gave all of the evaluators a checklist to score the firms. The next day, he called me to get my two finalists. I had only one: "Edelman. Everyone else was selling, but Edelman was **telling you how and why** you can lead your industry."

Implications and benefits:

▶ **Leaves a positive impression.** Telling feels more like a conversation, whereas selling becomes a presentation.

▶ **It encourages involvement.** When hearing a good story, you feel more engaged in the conversation.

▶ **It's respectful and professional.** People want to be treated well and not manipulated.

Where's the Disconnect? When a Story Is Missing

It can be frustrating for people to visit a company's website, read it, and leave without knowing what the company does. And that happens all too often—not just online, but in meetings, presentations, and conferences. Businesspeople talk but *say* nothing.

My cousin, a business consultant in New York, was approached by a recruiter to interview for an open executive position at another professional services firm. His first move was to go to the firm's site and do some reading to prepare for the interview. Flustered and confused, he called me to decipher what that company *really did*.

"It sounds like I'm missing the point, and maybe it's just me," he lamented on the phone, wondering if his skills matched their offering. "I thought, given your profession, you could spend some time on their site and figure it out for me."

"Forensic messaging isn't really my specialty," I thought, wondering how to help him out. While we were on the phone, I checked online for a few minutes to look for some clues. All I found was a laundry list of business buzzwords that didn't describe anything specifically; in fact, they just sounded like the company did what everyone else in technology consulting might claim to do.

"Mike, I think they're playing it safe and giving the laundry-list approach," I advised. "In my experience, they say they do everything and are really saying nothing. The only option for you is to do the first phone call with the CEO and ask a few open-ended questions."

"Like what?"

"Ask him for a few short examples of their best clients. Ask him who they sell to and why companies buy from him. Get him talking, and you'll probably get a clearer sense of what they do and if you're qualified for the open position."

"I'd really like to be better prepared before doing that," he said reluctantly.

"I know, but they're giving you a corporate smokescreen and there's no way to know what they do unless you get them to share a few success stories."

"Makes sense. I'll let you know what I hear."

Unfortunately, my cousin was likely not the only person to encounter such roadblocks. Companies do this all the time—say both everything and nothing at all. It drives regular people crazy.

Contrast my cousin's frustration with the clarity a boutique consulting firm in Chicago creates when it describes its organization in its website's About Us section. It consciously elected to tell a story about how its clients want to get their employees to embrace change but initially don't succeed.

What struck me instantly when I visited their site was the storyline's *simplicity*.

"There are executives that have a clear intention to change—the few—and there is a disconnect with the many who can enact it. The few envision the idea, and the many struggle to make it happen, and there's a chasm between them."

This made immediate sense to me—because the story grabs you and pulls you in. You begin to feel for the ineffectiveness of the few and the impotence of the many, and as a result, hope for resolution. We wonder, can the chasm be crossed?

That's the power of a good narrative: it speaks directly to you and creates instant clarity. It's memorable and easy to step into.

Like Apple, businesses that embrace stories can make quick connections that last. Those that feel stories aren't appropriate leave people hungry, confused, and irritated.

The Birth of Narrative Mapping: A Way to Organize and Deliver Your Story

Over the course of many years, I developed the following distinct methodology to organize and deliver corporate narratives.

Earlier in my career, I used basic visual mind maps called message maps in my workshops. I helped clients that ranged from large multinationals to start-ups develop an outline and gain consensus on their core message. They typically used these structures for public relations (PR) and media purposes.

During these mind-mapping exercises, small groups of 8 to 10 key stakeholders gathered in a room with a large whiteboard and some flip charts. They set about to openly tackle topics like industry issues, new product launches, and new corporate strategies. I promised that their message map would reflect a common understanding and help them craft a clear hierarchy of essential ideas. The results were strong visual outlines or key messages they all agreed to share.

I liked facilitating these sessions and leading disparate perspectives into a common way of explaining something tricky. I saw potential for the message maps not only to convey a company's key ideas but also to do more. Because I tend to think like a journalist, I started to evolve message maps to build a *story*—not just corporate talking points. I enjoyed seeing the narrative-like progression of those ideas develop and started to wonder how I might connect them in a more logical, visual way. I enjoyed these exercises so much that, in 2006, I decided to break off on my own and start a business so that I could dedicate myself exclusively to elevating and advancing the art of message mapping.

The following story is a good example of how I transformed maps of corporate talking points into more visual storytelling maps. I taught message maps to many people during my career, including U.S. Army Public Affairs leaders. On one occasion, I helped debrief General William Caldwell of the 82nd Airborne on his new assignment as the chief media spokesperson for Central Command in Iraq. When I eventually became Gen. Caldwell's media trainer, I saw him immediately embrace the tool, not only as a spokesperson in Iraq, but also as head of the Command and General Staff College, the Army's graduate school for officers, in Fort Leavenworth, Kansas.

Later, Gen. Caldwell invited me to speak at a senior leadership conference for Army generals on the power of narratives and message mapping. He also sanctioned research on the role of narratives as part of a more ambitious project to refine Army doctrine on how to share and disseminate information in what was then the new era of 24-hour media.

Gen. Caldwell's research team interviewed me extensively on message maps in Chicago. By this time, I fully realized how such a map could fuse with an organization's need for a common story. It was during those interviews that I first conceived the term "Narrative Map."

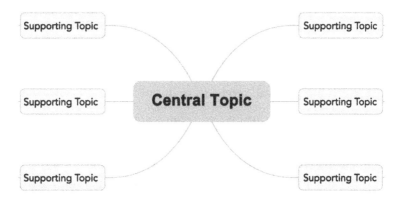

Rediscovery of Narratives and Storytelling: Breaking through the Blah, Blah, Blah

By this point, you've rediscovered (or finally realized) the vital role stories play in crafting clear and organized messages you want to share. You recognize that this was always welcome, yet often overlooked by many of your colleagues and peers in the business world.

Thankfully, organizations are beginning to notice that telling stories is a strategic way to manage people's attention. It's not only an acceptable business practice these days; it's the key to establishing a powerful, common, and lasting understanding.

When I read a good story, it sticks with me. Yet how many companies *tell* a good story? Most are eminently forgettable, usually because they all sound the same.

Some organizations, however, do have a great story. Take Southwest Airlines, for instance. Their employees look back and tell stories of how Herb Kelleher had a powerful vision for a new type of airline.

His narrative of a new airline that was thrifty, focused, and fun quickly spread. Their stock symbol was LUV. Their employees embraced the story every day—and still do.

Just as Apple reinvented the phone, Southwest reinvented the airplane flight.

Yet most businesses still don't get it. Having and sharing a good story, though logical, might seem out of reach.

Look at the state of business communication today. There's little clarity and discipline—something that becomes apparent when you attend any business conference. It lasts for a few days and features one presentation after another that bores you to tears.

It's very information-driven, like being lectured to hour after hour. It's cold and inhuman.

Stories are a more *human and respectful* way to communicate.

Many years ago, I had the privilege to hear Southwest's co-founder speak at an industry event. Everything about his speech was memorable—even manly. (Imagine that!) His entry was dramatic. A walk down the center aisle under an archway of flashlights used to guide aircraft to the gate held proudly by his employees—an emperor under the wild welcome of fun-loving colleagues.

Kelleher's dress was business casual at a time when all CEOs wore suits and ties. He even poured himself a scotch and smoked a cigarette during his speech. The approach was pure cowboy, and it perfectly matched the plain speaking and storytelling that held me captive. For 40 minutes, he told tales that illustrated the character and courage of his airline, which was setting a new standard in the industry.

I'm certain Kelleher was no lover of PowerPoint. His interactions were passionate and pointed. He told the Southwest Airlines story with pride.

Just a century ago, storytelling was a skill widely used. And although it's been mostly lost in the information age, people *still love* stories. We need to spread the love and learn to embrace—and engage in—solid storytelling.

Listen, I'm Ready for a Story

When you throw a party, you do your best to make it fun. However, this doesn't seem to be your concern when you have a big business meeting. Why are these meetings so boring?

A client of mine who works for a Fortune 500 manufacturing firm was holding a big two-day conference with his management team about a new initiative and requested my help. He was concerned about the last day of the conference because the executives were going to give speeches *all day long*.

I asked him, "Is there anything you can do that would make the agenda more interesting? We've got to be sensitive to people's time and their ability to pay attention for two days."

"Nothing, really," he admitted. "Everybody who is on this agenda has to speak, and they've all asked for 50 minutes with 10-minute breaks between the keynotes."

I could picture the managers in the crowd dropping like flies over the course of two full days of meetings. I imagined fidgeting, zone-outs, and hordes of attendees secretly checking their smartphones and having a nearly impossible time paying attention to the presentations.

"Can I suggest any way to alter the agenda?" I asked.

He said, "It's too late; they've already chosen the speakers, and there's nothing I can do."

My client recognized the problem as I did, but he threw his hands up.

"It's just how we've always done it," he said.

I felt terrible for the attendees. They would be energized about a new strategic initiative being announced on day one. Everyone would be actively participating in some hands-on training and practical sessions. Yet the grand finale would be the ultimate buzzkill.

"I have an idea that might lighten it up and make it more tolerable," I said. "Why don't you introduce each speaker with a short bio that highlights key aspects of his or her life, including education, hometown, hobbies, and alma mater? With that, you've created a little story on each of them." I suggested.

I went on, "We can find a short YouTube video clip from a movie or TV show that has some direct, yet offbeat, connection to their bio. This will give the audience moments of levity. For example, the head of sales gets a clip from *Tommy Boy*, the Chris Farley movie that depicts a guy who struggles to succeed his deceased father, a consummate dealmaker; or a *What about Bob* clip that shows a funny scene with Bill Murray strapped to a mast to make light of a woman who was a collegiate sailor."

The approach was a huge success. It helped the company turn a standard introduction into an interesting biography that sketched a brief story about each presenter. Each humorous short video was a personal parody. Months after the conference ended, people still remembered the video introductions.

[brief] BITS

Speak in headlines, or risk losing your audience.

"Dewey Defeats Truman." Headlines get people's attention and stay with them as much as an image. The headline is the hook that gets people to pick up the paper from the stand. When business people speak in headlines, they steal a page from journalism and frame a subject in a way that makes people want to hear more.

Think About Your Audience: Journalism 2.0 and the Elements of a Narrative

You're not a journalist, and you don't think like one—but you should. Anybody who regularly communicates important information and wants to get—and hold—people's attention can benefit from a crash course in journalism.

In college I discovered a love for reporting, particularly sports. I wrote news stories and, later, a weekly column. Thinking about what stories my classmates at Loyola University of Chicago would find interesting was a constant challenge. A friend of mine, Greg, who later worked at *Time* magazine and Fox News, taught me a great lesson: he was *always passionate* about breaking the big story.

Those precareer lessons from him got me thinking about how to win over an audience. Our conversations motivated me to consider a story's broader appeal, especially when I entered the world of brand communications and corporate strategy. What lessons could I transfer from journalism to the business world?

As it turns out, many of them.

On one occasion, I led a storytelling exercise with 200 executives at a global supply company. It was a leadership meeting that helped senior-level managers reduce a very long story to a 3-minute version. That exercise gave them the basic tools to summarize and streamline complexity into a cohesive narrative.

I was teaching a new strain of journalism, and they loved it.

From those workshops, key considerations of a great story emerged:

- Strong headline
- Compelling lead paragraph
- Clear sense of conflict
- Personal voice

- Consistent narrative thread
- Logical sequence of events
- Character development
- Powerful conclusion

And it must make sense, have a point, and come to a resolution.

We have a lot to learn from journalism's focus on the broader appeal of stories. Stories aren't just for news; they keep people connected. Just as a journalist does, we have to consider and respect the elements that make a good story. And as more and more organizations begin to recognize the value of this form of journalism, they must watch out for some common pitfalls that can turn a good story into a bad one.

The following is a short list of some of the early warning signs that occur when organizations misinterpret how and when to use storytelling to their best advantage.

Warning #1: Keep Stories Short

You have to be sure to limit a story's length. When you begin to learn and embrace this process, you may become overly excited and start to get long-winded. That's a natural reaction when you find a new tool that trumps boring and obtuse corporate-speak and makes your business human and interesting again.

When you start to fall (back) in love with storytelling, there's an inevitable danger of holding the audience's attention *too long*. Ironically, narratives solve one problem but might create a new one.

Keep them short and to the point.

Your presentation gets lost

▶ If you don't get to the point, they'll choose their smartphone over you. Don't let that happen.

Warning #2: Don't Fall in Love with Fables and "Once upon a Time"

Sometimes people embrace the broader and more esoteric concept of the art form, exploring the intricate theories of narrative, fables, satire, and even the power of myth. What's more, some companies fear storytelling because they think it turns serious business issues into playtime or that it's going to somehow weaken the gravity of their message.

We're not talking about "Once upon a time" here. We're talking about a corporate narrative that explains why, how, who, when, where, and so what. These stories must tackle and decode business issues, strategic decisions, new trends, and complex market dynamics—while making all of it personal and intelligible. They are stories like Apple's or Southwest Airlines'—seriously successful ideas that are presented in a human way. Be wary when you hear people talk about Joseph Campbell or *Star Wars;* you want to keep it simple. Tell a story that makes it easier to explain something vital.

Warning #3: Don't Just *Promote* Storytelling; *Teach* It

Storytelling is a powerful tool. As such, it needs to be taught.

Some companies jump onto the narrative bandwagon and start to call every type of communication a story. Yet many people don't have a proper understanding of how to translate information into a compelling narrative form. What's more, people start sharing stories without knowing how to keep them tight.

One of my clients recognized the huge opportunity that lay before his company in having its management team master storytelling. So, I partnered with a small change management firm to design a customized Story Streaming workshop to help this client's team grasp the basic elements of building and sharing stories.

The workshops were engaging and easy to embrace. Managers were given a topic and put in small teams of four to stream their stories. Each of them received a workbook and tools to help chart the source, stream, tributaries, and delta of their story.

"It was powerful to see managers turn boring, long-winded topics into tight story streams," said the lead facilitator. "Hearing them weeks later 'stream' their stories meant that they knew how to convert corporate-speak into something short, sweet, and to the point."

If you promote storytelling but fail to teach it, you'll only frustrate and confuse people. Giving them the skills to structure and share a solid story can go a long way in their brevity development. It not only helps them professionally; it also shows them how a narrative's conciseness can personalize their jobs.

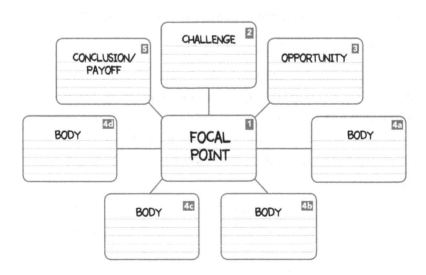

Narrative Map (De)constructed

Narrative Maps consist of several important elements that make it easier to explain messages and give them clarity and context.

Let me illustrate this by going back to Steve Jobs's iPhone launch as an example of how to map a strategic narrative.

Narrative Maps have a *clockwise build*. You start with the center bubble and add bubbles around it clockwise.

- *Focal point* (center bubble): This is the central part of a narrative. It's akin to a headline and explains and isolates the point of the story: Is it about innovation, change, competition, or something else?

- *Setup or challenge* (the bubble directly above the focal point): What challenge, conflict, or issue exists in the marketplace that your organization is addressing? Why does this problem exist, and who contributes to it? This begins to isolate within the story the major issue.

- *Opportunity* (moving clockwise, the bubble to the top right): What is the implication or the opportunity for your organization? This is what some people call an unmet need or an aha moment; something that you could do to begin to effect change or to address and resolve an issue.

- *Approach* (continuing to move clockwise around the center bubble, the three or four bubbles moving around the focal point): How does your story unfold? What are the three or four characters or key elements? What is the *how, where,* or *when?*

- *Payoff* (the bubble to the top left of the focal point): All good stories have a conclusive end-state or payoff. How do you resolve the set up from the beginning? For example, let's say that the story is about innovation, and there are four ways in which the company is going to innovate. How is that going to benefit somebody? Where does the story conclude? Who feels the benefits?

When you translate boring business speak into a Narrative Map, you apply a filter that makes it interesting.

Narrative Mapping synthesizes volumes of information into a visual outline that produces a logical, strategic, highly contextual, and relevant story. It's also credible because your organization firmly believes the story is true and will have an impact on people, and it's concise because it's on one page.

If you map out your narrative, you could use that story to talk to a client or share it with a room full of key audiences, such as investors, partners, and employees. And you could have people nodding their heads in real understanding in less than 5 minutes.

Seeing and Hearing Is Believing: The Story of the Evolution of Commerce

One of my clients is a company that processes credit card transactions and provides a broad set of technologies for financial institutions and merchants. The company had reached a defining moment: it was planning to roll out a new set of products for the financial services market that went far beyond processing a financial transaction. However, the company did not have internal agreement about the essence of the message, so its management called me for help to build a Narrative Map and uncover the underlying story.

This initiative, called Universal Commerce, was about the evolution of commerce. But there was some debate within the company about the name: Was that term really about an industry trend or a set of products?

I led them through a Narrative Mapping session. I called a dozen key stakeholders into a room, where they discussed this challenge and topic in full detail. They started thinking about it as a story, piecing it together.

They asked themselves, "What's driving this change?" We mapped that topic out and isolated key points on the whiteboard map. In the end, we rolled it up into a one-page Narrative Map that outlined the client's entire story—a great one that explained how the way people do business has evolved over the years. It tracked how we've gone from traditional commerce, in which we go to a store and buy a product; to e-commerce, in which we go online and buy a product; to now, when smartphones and mobile devices allow us to shop wherever we are, and customers expect a completely integrated experience.

The story affects consumers and merchants in an immediate way. Specifically, consumers have a heightened expectation that technology is like magic and that these devices are going to work together and be highly personalized.

We took that story and turned it into a short video animation of hand-drawn illustrations on a whiteboard, which we called a whiteboard narrative. In this form, a narrator explains the story while it's being hand-drawn in an accelerated time-lapse animation with music.

It took a few weeks to get the story straight. However, if we hadn't translated this message into a Narrative Map, it might have been very confusing, with the potential to mislead their executives and sales force. They would have missed the potential beauty and brilliance of this cohesive perspective and ruined any chance of a good story.

The day before the big presentation to the sales force, the leadership team was rehearsing the whiteboard video in a meeting room at a convention center. They showed the short narrative animation to the company's CEO. At the end, he turned to the senior executive who was leading this initiative and said simply, "*I get it.*"

He had *thought* he understood the strategy—until he saw the presentation. Now, it was truly crystal clear to him.

That narrative solidified a common and deep level of under-standing among thousands of people. Here's what they heard:

"This is a story of commerce—how the way we buy is chang-ing. Consumers today want it all; they expect to get the best deal in the most convenient and personalized way and to be connected anywhere, all the time. At our company, we call this Universal Commerce.

For a long time, people didn't have much control over how, when, and where they shopped. They would visit a store and deter-mine whether they were willing to pay the asking price. Then came e-commerce, which brought greater power and choice. Buying online or in a store, however, were initially very different expe-riences. The more recent emergence of smart, connected mobile devices merged these two worlds and created mCommerce.

The convergence of offline shopping and e-commerce through mCommerce has created a new world of Universal Commerce where consumers expect a more integrated buying experience that's quick and consistent wherever they are and at any time.

Imagine this: Your neighbor needs to buy a birthday present for his daughter. He gets an e-mail alert with a recommended deal on a jacket. He looks the jacket up, reads reviews online, checks pricing, and places the item with the best price in his virtual shop-ping cart. Later, as he approaches his local mall while running errands, he gets an alert on his smartphone that one of the stores has it in stock and will give him a better price if he gets it now. At checkout, he selects his credit card in his mobile wallet and waves to pay using his loyalty points.

As he continues his errands, he pulls up the Starbuck's app on his phone to order his favorite latte. On his way, he selects his preferred payment method from his phone and when he arrives the drink is waiting on the counter and already paid for. He walks past the line, grabs his drink, and leaves, all in under a minute.

In a reality of increasing consumer expectations, payments are lagging behind. To become and remain relevant, merchants and financial institutions need to adapt quickly. So how will they keep pace with such rapid change and deliver a completely integrated experience?

The age of Universal Commerce is already upon us, full of promise and potential.

And in a world of endless options, we can make it all possible."

That story has a significant and personal appeal to every audience that hears it. The salesperson knows how to explain and sell this vision to customers, consumers feel this company understands their needs, financial institutions see that this company understands how technology is changing people's lives, merchants want this company to help them because they understand how they need to adapt to consumers' expectations, and analysts pay closer attention to the company, because it's leading an evolution of commerce.

This story has power and purpose.

Long story, short. People are buried in corporate-speak, but you can help them by embracing narrative storytelling to be clear, concise, and compelling.

8 Talk It: Controlled Conversations and TALC Tracks

Long story, short. To be brief means to avoid endless mono-logues and to start having controlled conversations with a rhythm, a purpose, and a point.

Some people think that brevity means killing off conversa-tions altogether. This is neither true nor my intention in writing this book.

In fact, just the opposite is true. Real brevity invites and encourages really good, meaningful, *controlled conversations*. By that, I mean two people talking willingly—and enjoying it—but not feeling the conversation has to last forever to be worthwhile.

A controlled conversation is a disciplined conversation. What you're talking about matters to the person you're talking to, and your active listening tells you what matters to that person. You have the other person's interest and assent.

Controlled conversations make you feel free to stop at any time and not risk alienating anybody or feeling awkward. One example is talking to people on airplanes.

Risky Business Trip

When I travel, I frequently start conversations with people on flights and have terrific—and always brief—conversations with them that are both engaging and don't last the entire trip. However, this is a nightmare scenario for many people, especially on longer flights where you are a captive audience, and *especially* if you are seated (trapped, in fact) in a window seat.

What's my trick? Active listening. For a trip to Spain, here's what it might sound like:

"So why are you going to Spain?" I start.

"Well, I am going to a medical conference," he answers.

"Where is it?" I ask.

"It's in Barcelona," he responds.

At this point, I can take the conversation in many different directions by saying just a little and asking good questions that I think will lead to shorter answers—or, none at all.

I avoid three common mistakes that draw people into long, unwieldy conversations:

1. *Passive listening*: Let the other person ramble on about everything and say nothing (result: no control).

2. *Waiting my turn*: Let the person talk and then jump in to say my part (result: two conversations).

3. *Impulsively reacting*: Respond to a word or thought the person has said (result: no clear direction).

What's most important is to make the conversation *about the other person* by asking thoughtful and intentional questions centered on him or her. This allows you to stay in control; because you find out what's important to *him or her*, you can converse confidently.

━ [brief] BASICS ━━━━━━━━━━━━━━━━━━━━━━━━━━━

CHECKING IN:
KNOW WHAT THEY'RE THINKING

Pausing to check in with your audience gets you to stop talking and lets you know if people are paying attention and tracking what you are saying.

You're with a group of friends at an incredibly busy restaurant on a Friday night. After waiting a long time for a table, you are finally seated. You expect to see the server shortly, but a few minutes turn into 10, and you start to fume. Your waitress finally arrives and apologizes. You place your drink order—and wait. You place your dinner order—and **wait** some more.

At some point, the long wait becomes the only topic of conversation, as you all start complaining about the poor service. When the manager arrives and asks, **"How's everything?"** you give him an earful. He then expedites the process and takes a nice chunk off the bill.

The manager did something called **checking in**—and it's the only way to know what a customer thinks. It not only gets you to stop talking; it also allows you to tell whether people are **tracking** what you are saying. It's your lifeline, yet it's rarely employed. Why? Maybe you really don't want to know, so you dread asking. But the benefits are many:

▶ **You'll be understood.** Most people mistakenly assume what they say is clear. Instead, be convinced that the audience gets easily lost. Your primary concern is to ask good, open-ended questions to ensure they're on the same page.

▶ **It ensures you're clear and concise.** By pausing periodically, you're not only trimming; you're also testing whether they get it. If you don't ask, they won't tell.

▶ **It eliminates monologues.** If you don't check in, they'll check out.

DING!

Controlled Conversations Are a Game of Tennis, Not Golf

Talking isn't like a round of golf, in which each player takes turns and waits for the next shot. Talking is more like tennis; it's about active listening, asking good questions, and bantering back and forth. After a while, a balanced rhythm emerges.

Thus, brevity becomes possible when you have *one* conversation, *not two*, and you can control its direction, cadence, and flow. And you accomplish this by doing something incredibly rare: *listening*. When you aren't talking as much, you're making the conversation more about the other person.

After a short while, the person next to you starts enjoying the conversation because they're doing a fair share of the talking, but not all of it. You ask questions based on interest, and you control the frequency of the questions and comments.

"So why did you go to the conference in Madrid?" I ask because I'm interested in knowing a little more.

"I am a brain surgeon," he responds.

If I wanted the conversation to continue, I would ask a gateway question, such as, "Where did you go to medical school?"

If I want the conversation to end so I can catch a few winks on the flight or read my book, I politely say, "Oh, that's interesting," and stop asking questions. The pause lets me control the conversation.

TALC Tracks—A Structure for Balance and Brevity

TALC Tracks—talk, active listening, converse—are a tactic for organizing almost any exchange in a powerful way to keep it brief and memorable. The TALC approach is not a formula; it is an adjustable method that helps you track the ideas your conversation partner shares and project interesting paths for the conversation to follow. It doesn't just call on the techniques of mapping or story-telling; it's about having a balanced, controlled conversation. Let's look at each part in detail.

- *T, or talk*: Somebody starts talking. Let that person say what he or she is going to say. Don't worry if it lasts 1 minute or 5; just let the person talk.

    Two keys for you to consider:

    ◆ Be prepared to say something when the other person finishes speaking.

    ◆ Make sure your response has a clear point.

- *AL, or actively listen*: Closely listen to what the other person is saying with interest the *entire* time. Don't zone out or multitask or get distracted trying to think of a response. Listen for key words, names, dates, and even a basic narrative thread. It's not *easy listening*, like letting smooth jazz wash over you without much thought or consideration; it's *active*, because you're involved in the next step of the conversation. Think about how and when you'll chime in. This way, you're ready to participate when your turn comes.

Two keys for you to consider:

- Ask open-ended questions that are connected to what you've heard.

- Tap into the parts of the topic you're genuinely interested in.

- *C, or converse*: When a natural pause comes, jump in and comment, question, or even bridge to a different topic that's related to what's being said. Contribute to building *one* conversation.

   Three keys for you to consider:

   - Do not use your turn to start an irrelevant conversation.

   - Keep your responses short.

   - Know when to end so the other person can begin talking again.

Be Prepared for Anything

So what does the concept of the controlled conversation and TALC Tracks mean to you?

It means that you'll be prepared for conflict or agreement. You can keep a conversation on point and represent your agenda effectively while respecting what someone else has to say.

─ [brief] BASICS ─

ACTIVE LISTENING:
KNOWING WHAT MATTERS TO PEOPLE
Active listening helps you determine what matters to your audience.

Active listening helps you determine what matters to your audience. The people that I work with at U.S. Special Operations are among the most talented, dedicated, and committed professionals I have ever met. They not only risk their lives to protect their fellow citizens but also make remarkable sacrifices to raise their game in every aspect of their profession. As learners, they are off the charts.

Surprisingly, however, nearly all of them openly admit in our courses that they are **terrible listeners**. In fact, I haven't met one who professes it to be one of their strengths.

Active listening is a fundamental skill for achieving brevity. It's somewhat ironic, given that brevity is often assumed to be about only cutting down what's communicated. But it's what you hear **when not speaking** that helps you determine what matters to your audience. Some components of active listening are:

▶ **It lets you synthesize and summarize.** It allows you not only to hear mounds of information but also to distill and package it into strong summaries that people value.

▶ **It makes you more human.** With greater empathy comes concern and attention.

▶ **It prevents you from talking too much.** Asking good questions and listening well lessens your risk of being long-winded.

▶ **It invites conversations.** Great active listeners ask questions that get other people talking more.

When I think about it, 80 percent of the conversations I have with my coworkers are just simple, enjoyable exchanges. But 20 percent of the time, we have a controlled conversation—one in which I am applying brevity and balance to mitigate some of the instinctual or emotional problems I have when I talk about important or stressful topics.

Active listening plays a big role in controlled conversation. It helps me gauge the other person's mind-set and what matters to him or her. Do not forget to leave time for the *other person* to listen, too; he or she needs a chance to track and engage as much as you do.

Audience, Audience, Audience

The whole idea of being brief is about knowing what's important to the people you're talking with. Focusing on their priorities means that you respect them, what they say, how they listen, and their valuable time.

That doesn't mean you don't have an agenda or goals for your conversation. Rather, it's simply more effective for your agenda to focus on them first. Controlled conversation isn't about controlling *the conversation* as much as it is controlling *yourself* in the conversation. That is what will make you an effective communicator.

[brief] **BITS**

Pauses are a strong weapon for brevity.

[FIRE AWAY!]

Paul Harvey was a masterful radio announcer who used a few devices to hold an audience's attention during his radio showcase called *The Rest of the Story*. He held people's attention not only by skillfully telling a story but also by knowing when to pause. Silence is a momentary magnet that draws an audience in with what isn't said. Harvey concluded each segment "And...now...you know (pause) the *rest* of the story."

> ► The consequences of information overload can be disastrous and a burden to carry. Lighten their load.

For example, think about people who push and post tons of irrelevant or trivial content on social media. Not only is it annoying; it hurts their reputation as an objective source of information.

The opposite of that—and someone whose online content I admire—is business adviser Brad Farris, a BRIEF social media guy (https://twitter.com/blfarris). His posts, although occasional, always have high value. He knows his followers get hit with waves of content online every day, and he respects their time by sharing *only what's important.*

Even if I had a slightly different agenda than him during a conversation, I would not mind spending time on his point of view, because he's earned it. He gives me information that is disciplined, relevant, and respectful.

Brevity breeds better conversations—that point is clear.

Long story, short. To be brief means to avoid endless monologues and to start having controlled conversations with a rhythm, a purpose, and a point.

9 Show It: Powerful Ways to Make a Picture Exceed a Thousand Words

Long story, short. Visual communications are far more appealing than words alone. Explore simple, more effective ways that prove a picture's worth a thousand words.

Show-and-Tell: Which Would You Choose?

When you think about showing what you mean, always consider the audience members' perspective. Which of these would you choose if you were them?

- A textbook with 500 pages filled with words or one with graphs, images, and diagrams?

- A three-page paid advertisement filled with text and a boring stock image or an online guide of interactive diagrams and video?

- A PowerPoint slide with 10 bullets or one with one strong image and a catchy title?

- An e-mail you scroll down three screens to finish reading or a link to a 1-minute video animation that simplifies it?

- A mobile phone with monochrome green or a smartphone with flashy icons?

- A presenter who simply reads the slides or one who draws throughout?

- A talking head video or a video with personal interviews, actual footage, and a real story?

These are the choices you make *first* so that your audience can get what you're saying, easier and faster. If you do the hard work up front, your audience won't have to pay the price later.

You Can See the Shift

We are transitioning from a text-based world to a visual one. Screens and interactive media pervade all parts of our lives. Screens are in our homes, our classrooms, our elevators, even our bathrooms. They have replaced phones, books, newspapers, billboards, and printed menus.

Some of the most popular types of social media are visually based: Pinterest, Tumblr, Instagram, and Vine. Now more than ever, people expect the information they encounter on a day-to-day basis to interact, evolve, and engage. We are living in the age of infographics—compact and appealing visual interpretations of verbal or numerical data. Nowadays, media such as videos, infographics, illustrations, and animations all take center stage.

According to many studies, 65 percent of the population learns visually. Furthermore, studies show that whereas we remember only 10 percent of what we hear and 30 percent of what we read, we remember a whopping 80 percent of what we see. Given this appetite, there is an enormous opportunity for visual communication to increase the effectiveness and brevity of how we communicate.

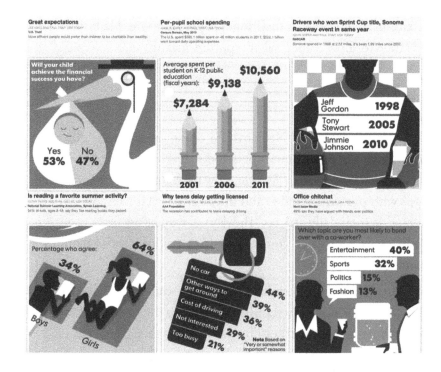

Seeing Supersedes Reading

People's preference for seeing over reading is more important than ever. We can look to *USA Today* founder Al Neuharth, who redefined journalism in the 1980s with his radically different take on newspapers, as an example of this.

After analyzing how people read newspapers at that time, Neuharth decided there needed to be an easier way to consume the daily news. As a result, *USA Today* stories are short, rarely jump to a second page, and use lots of visuals. Neuharth's emphasis on the visual even created the cottage industry of infographics.

Neuharth wasn't a newspaper purist. Rather, he belongs in the BRIEF Hall of Fame. He recognized the permanent shift from text to visuals and realized that people just don't have the time or attention span to read a traditional paper anymore. He knew it was time to show readers what reporters meant.

A Visual Language

While people criticized Neuharth for doing this in the 1980s, he has influenced major newspapers and magazines today. Many, including the *Wall Street Journal*, now have smartphone and tablet apps with prominent video and interactive visual components alongside their daily articles. The days of text-heavy news pages are over. For *all* industries, communicating effectively today requires communicating visually.

But it's difficult; after all, not everyone can easily make an infographic or naturally translate a narrative into a concise and compelling graph, chart, or illustration. Less than 3 percent of companies use visual communication, precisely because it's difficult to get it right. It's easier to write than to find the right image worth 1,000 words. But making that extra effort up front makes all the difference when people pick up the report and *understand* exactly what we're saying. To communicate our ideas visually, we need to engage both sides of our brain: the logical left and the creative right.

Although a headline might help, Paul Stannard, founder and CEO of SmartDraw, explains that communicating with images is six times more effective than with words alone. He estimates that more unique information will be formed in one year today than in the past 5,000 years.

It truly is like learning to speak a different language.

When I first started Sheffield, one of my clients—Swedish software company CogMed—wanted to market its new software designed to help educate people with attention-deficit disorder (ADD). Its managers approached me because they wanted to extract a narrative for the U.S. market about the benefits of exercising working memory for people with noticeable cognitive limitations.

As you might imagine, the neuroscientists who designed this software are brilliant. But they were struggling to find a way to hold their audience's attention more than ever. After all, their potential customers had ADD.

So we turned to infographic genius John Telford. We simplified the information on the new software down to three points, and translated it into a one-page visual story. It was like speaking into an automatic visual translating machine.

"I use myself and the people I work with as test cases. It's the ability to look at things from a different perspective than those who are immersed in it," Telford said. "When I make an infographic, I'm saying, 'Here's how to explain the idea to someone who has no idea what you're talking about, in the simplest terms.' I can show it in a way that laymen can understand, because I am one of those people."

Telford knew both languages, the verbal and the visual, and, like magic, he helped turn our verbal narrative into meaningful images.

"It's a way of looking at information and being able to dissect it," Telford said. "There are a lot of experts who can throw information at you, but the trick is getting somebody who isn't familiar with the concept to understand the essence."

It did the trick and helped CogMed tell the story visually.

Connect an Image with Your Story

Infographic designers need to first understand the essential point of what they are trying to communicate. This is the easy part. The hard part is finding a correlating visual that explains the story with images.

During the severe recession in 2008, I worked with some business executives who wanted me to present to a leadership team about the potential challenges inherent in communicating to employees during tough times. The economic slump was scary; some even compared it to the Great Depression.

I certainly did not know what it was like to live in the 1930s, but my dad used to tell me a story about my grandmother when she worked as a seamstress for Sears Roebuck in Chicago. Her job was to sew buttons on jackets all day long. Her secret for staying employed during the Depression was, if she finished her work before the day was over, she would go back and tear off all the buttons, and start all over again. Her mantra was "Make sure they always see you working."

So I decided to use this story in my presentation. For my visual, I searched "jacket with buttons" on Google, put it on one slide, and told my story within 15 minutes. It was that simple. I identified the point I wanted to make and did a modest amount of visual research. This powerful pairing of the verbal and visual really worked.

Just do the hard work up front. It will have an enormous payoff for the audience on the back end.

Here are some easy ways to jump into the visual world.

1. Google images that relate to your presentation.

2. Draw during your presentations.

3. Find short videos online.

4. Make short videos of your own.

5. Use a whiteboard to illustrate.

6. Bring in small items for show-and-tell lessons.

7. Look into prezi.com for a different kind of presentation.

8. Show stunning photography instead of words.

9. Color-code your memos.

10. Substitute icons for frequently used words.

Momentary Magic: Infographics in Business

Visual communication distills complex information, explains it, makes it entertaining, and most importantly, makes it easy to consume. Mastering this art can immediately impact how you communicate highly complex ideas, both internally and externally.

Take, for example, what some publicly traded organizations such as GE, Sears, Walmart, and Apple do when they need an annual report for their shareholders. Annual reports usually have a lot of charts, images, and graphs to make it easier for the shareholder to understand the company's current and predicted status. It's almost a mini-magazine with a target, niche audience that doesn't necessarily have all the time or background to deal with the raw data.

A lot of companies miss the mark, however, because although they include pictures to break up the text, these images don't tell the *specific story* of the state of the organization.

You need to assume people won't read what you write. The same cohesive story should appear in both the text and the illustration.

Breakdown of Complex Information

The Power of Infographics author Mark Smiciklas explains that 50 percent of our brain is dedicated to visual function.[1] But even though we have an innate preference to learn visually, very few businesses choose to appease their customer's appetite for visual information. For example, Monitise, a mobile money solutions provider, took out an ad in the *Wall Street Journal* digital edition that screamed, "Please, don't read this, because we don't know how to lead in today's technological world." The ad had only straight text and one uninteresting stock photo. It was like reading something in an outdated textbook. Talk about a dud. The potentially interactive experience fell completely flat, and their website was no better. The site had twice as many whitepapers as it did videos. Nothing about their ads or website demonstrated their services in a way that was visual or appealing.

One business that does visual communication right is marketing automation company Eloqua. Smiciklas describes how this organization uses infographics well to help people understand the dynamics of the online marketing space, often to explain the complexities of its software.

IKEA revolutionized the use of infographics in the furniture business. Anyone who's ever purchased something from the Swedish company knows that there are no words when you open up any of IKEA's assembly manuals—just pictures. They depict a person with an Allen wrench, illustrate the parts, and show how the furniture is put together. It's an intuitive, semipainless way to build your own furniture.

The Age of YouTube and Business

Video storytelling is becoming a more prominent way not only to educate and market but also to entertain and engage audiences.

People share tens of thousands of YouTube videos every day. Companies around the world are creating their own YouTube or Vimeo channels to tell their story visually. They recognize that if a picture is worth a thousand words, then a video is worth a million. But as with any form of communication, when you create a video, you must be highly sensitive to your audience.

You want to keep videos short. The average video on YouTube is about 3.5 minutes; after that amount of time, people start to lose interest and click away. The longer the video, the more difficult it is for people to pay attention all the way through.

For instance, a colleague sent me the link to a video of an expert in online marketing campaigns. It was free to watch, so I opened it. The first thing I looked at was the counter in the bottom right hand corner of the video clip telling me runtime.

This particular video lasted 15 minutes. That's longer than I like to watch, but my colleague gave such an enthusiastic endorsement of this guy that I clicked play. I got through 3 minutes, and then I began to wonder if I was interested enough to hang in for the full 15 minutes. After 3 minutes, the video lost my undivided attention, even though I was prepared to be fully engaged and interested in it.

[brief] **BITS**

Lean communicators have the muscle to trim what weighs them down.

[DROP &
GIVE ME
20!]

Will Strunk famously warned, "Omit needless words." If a person is drowning, don't add another ounce of water. Treat brevity as responsibility, empathy, and respect; become a lean communicator. Imagine if you had something important to share with someone who was running out the door to catch a train with very little time to spare. Treat all people like that, even when they're not in a hurry.

Be mindful of the time *and* the quality. If your videos have an amateurish feel, you will lose your audience immediately.

Another idea is to offer episodic videos. YouTube and Vimeo offer channels for corporations to create a series. If your videos are short and engaging and have educational and entertainment value, people may even look forward to the next episode in your series, as they do with their favorite television show. You want to think more like a broadcaster and less like a marketer.

Smartphone cameras also make creating video content even more convenient—as evidenced by the following story about Charlie Meyerson, a radio broadcaster who uses his iPhone to shoot live events and post on his blog. Meyerson was walking through Daley Plaza in Chicago and saw a young African American boy giving an impassioned speech about school closings in the city. He quickly began recording the boy on his smartphone and posted 2 minutes of his speech with a little intro on his blog. This kid could very well be the future mayor of Chicago.

Videos are very powerful tools to capture short, punchy messages and are easy to share.

TL; DR: Too Long; Didn't Read

You might be thinking, "I need to start creating infographics and shooting video right away." But an even simpler, powerful way of improving your visual communication is simple document formatting.

Format is crucial for any written material, be it a report, an e-mail, or a book. Traditional business books don't have graphics—but that trend is changing. If there are just words in a 100- to 150-page book in this day and age, it disregards the audience's strong visual preferences. Only an arrogant author would expect you to read the book cover to cover to figure out what he's trying to say. He should have the courtesy to summarize in many ways the moral of his story with images.

Take the time to prepare

► Have a plan before you speak, so everything is clear, concise and to the point. They will notice your effort and love it.

TL; DR—too long; didn't read—is the response of today's generation when messages fail to meet its expectation of brevity. This applies to e-mails, posts, and even books.

Here are a couple ways of making your written communication shorter and more appealing:

- *Make it inviting.* Deliver a strong title or subject line that's your invitation.

- *Limit your e-mail to the original window.* Your message is too long if the recipient has to scroll down to read it.

- *Embrace the white space.* Make sure there's white space and balance throughout the text. Instead of 8- to 10-sentence paragraphs, make them three to four sentences with returns in between.

- *Make it bold.* If you have a key idea in a document, call it out by making it bold.

- *Use bullets and numbers.* Start each point with a strong word or catchy phrase.

- *Cut the fluff.* Trim what's unnecessary, leaving a consumable and concise size.

The format, length, and layout of your text indicates if what's inside is amazing—or not worth their time.

The question on everyone's mind right now is, "Can you show me?" Pictures, animation, and infographics make complex, convoluted, lengthy ideas accessible and consumable for people. Satisfy this expectation, and train your audience to come back for more.

Long story, short. Visual communications are far more appealing than words alone. Explore simple, more effective ways that prove a picture's worth a thousand words.

10 Putting Brevity to Work: Grainger and the AI and Betty Story

L ong story, short. W. W. Grainger dared to be different by deciding to map, tell, talk, and show its five-year vision as a strategic narrative all employees could embrace.

One of the most compelling cases that combines mapping, telling, talking, and showing is how W. W. Grainger, a Fortune 500 industrial distributor headquartered in suburban Chicago, turned a complicated strategy into a simple story.

When I met with Grainger's head of strategic planning, John Borta, over coffee, I told him his company could use a narrative to simplify its complex business strategies.

"A lightbulb immediately went off for me when we started talking about how our senior leadership team could use Narrative Mapping to synthesize our five-year strategic vision," John said. "The thought of a strategic narrative was appealing, because it might help us speak to a broader base of managers and employees."

Grainger had spent the two prior years extensively studying market dynamics, key customer considerations, and how the company could tackle a much larger opportunity.

"We had literally *mounds* of research, insights, data, and recommendations that were rolled into lengthy presentations and detailed documentation," Borta told me. "It was the right plan, but we were really struggling to find a simpler way of talking about the vision without losing everyone in the process. The stakes were high."

So John had me come to a senior leadership team meeting at Grainger where the top dozen leaders of the U.S. organization were talking about finalizing and rolling out their five-year strategic vision. I led them in building a Narrative Map to explain the plan as a clear, concise, and compelling story.

During the 4-hour mapping session, I asked them questions about their planning process, the market, and key insights.

"Who are your customers?" I asked.

The response: "We really think we have two different customers: a janitor and a finance person."

I drew two columns with stick figures on the whiteboard.

"Okay, so let's call the janitor customer A and the accountant customer B to make it easier," I said. But rather than call them A and B, I named them Al and Betty. It made it simpler and more personal.

The attendees quickly rattled off the attributes of each customer type, and I jotted the descriptions under two columns.

We discussed what mattered to these two customers and how they were different.

"Al is a janitor who would buy products from Grainger, the Grainger catalog, the branches, and online. He has a ton of work to do and is worried about saving time when he needs a critical part or support service—like a screw, lightbulb, pump, or specialty item to keep the facility up and running and safe."

Words such as *time, convenience*, and *quality* appeared under Al's list.

"Betty is more of an accountant or finance person. She creates and approves purchase orders. She lives in a spreadsheet and runs the budget," they told me. "She works in the back office and cares about saving the company money."

We write *value* and *price* beneath Betty.

Over the next few hours, the senior leadership team developed a story around Al and Betty to explain their five-year strategic vision. When they finished mapping the narrative on a large whiteboard, their strategic vision was logically outlined in a simple and concise way.

"Everyone was on the same page, and they were excited to share the story," John told me.

Rolling the story out to the top 200 managers was the first challenge. The next was to explain it simply to that group.

The leadership team opted to abandon the traditional PowerPoint approach. Instead, it decided to draw pictures and have a conversation with the managers.

Grainger's president, Mike Pulick, stood up in front of the 200 managers and said: "We have a story that we want to share with you that's challenging and exciting. It explains what really matters to our customers and how we're going to help them."

"Let's start with what's at the heart of our strategy." With that, Pulick took out a blank sheet of paper and placed it in an old-school document projector, like the one you might have seen in a high school biology class. He used a marker to draw a circle, which was the focal point of the Narrative Map. Inside it he drew a picture of a first-place ribbon: the point of it all—to be the customer's first choice.

He handed the marker to one of his team members, who drew the next picture and the next part of the map. And so on. There were pictures of a clock and money, stick figures of Al and Betty, and other basic images. This was how they revealed their five-year strategic vision.

"People were transfixed," Borta recalled. "The leadership team never spoke so clearly and simply before. It was powerful and held the audience's attention for 40 minutes. And we didn't use one slide."

Then, as a challenge, Mike grabbed another blank piece of paper and a marker and placed them under the lone light of the document camera. He asked for a volunteer to come up and explain the company's five-year strategic vision to test the managers' understanding.

So one of the managers got up, took the blank piece of paper, and redrew the pictures and explained the strategic vision. She absolutely nailed it and told the story perfectly in less than 2 minutes. Everyone gave her a roaring round of applause and a standing ovation.

The story of Al and Betty captured the company's imagination. People immediately understood the strategy—what the plan was, why they were needed, whom they served, what made them special, and how they would deliver it.

And the most crucial part was that everybody there not only got it; they could *tell* it. As a result, 200 leaders went back and told their teams—and the story spread.

BE ALL IN:
PASSION AND ENERGY

Enthusiasm can be contagious—and a conscious business decision.

I had the opportunity to help a CEO reintroduce his company to a group of skeptical industry analysts. It had been a decade since his technology distribution firm had made a concerted effort to keep these market influencers properly informed.

After **tightening** his corporate narrative and **recalibrating** his presentation, we headed to a meet-and-greet at IDC, a leading research firm in Boston. He and I met some of the key players, and every time someone asked, "How's business?" he would tell his story with clarity and **enthusiasm**. The narrative we had mapped out was firmly in his head and heart.

He told his story of transformation and pulled them all in. Small introductions turned into longer conversations.

Between introductions, I said to him, "I thought you'd save that for the briefings tomorrow." He replied, "I decided to start tonight. We've got **a great story** to tell, and I didn't want to wait."

Implications:

► **Make a decision to commit.** If you're not all in, your audience won't be either; they care more about how you say it than what you're saying.

► **Spread excitement and enthusiasm; they're contagious.** You can get people on board if they see and feel that you're leading the way.

► **Remember that passion isn't always a sentiment.** Mature professionals decide to communicate with belief regardless of how they're feeling.

That was a defining moment for Grainger, and its impact continues to grow. *Harvard Business Review* cited the Al and Betty story, and the company's employees continue to talk about these two characters.[1] It helps them focus on the strategy and do what matters for them.

The employees recreated stick figures of Al and Betty on their own, and referred to Al and Betty in later presentations. Somebody made Al and Betty jewelry, and others left a chair for Al or Betty at meetings. They even created a music video.

Now, everybody asks, "How would this help Al?" and "How would this serve Betty?"

Al and Betty compelled more than 13,000 U.S. employees to think about how they can personally and simply connect with similar customers.

Grainger's strategic vision was sticky because it was presented as a *brief story*. The example of Al and Betty reflects how mapping, telling, talking, and showing can all work hand in hand as powerful tools to ensure brevity and effectiveness.

Long story, short. W. W. Grainger dared to be different by deciding to map, tell, talk, and show its five-year vision as a strategic narrative all employees could embrace.

Part Three
Decisiveness

Gaining the Decisiveness to Know When and Where to Be Brief

11 Meeting You Halfway

If you had to identify, in one word, the reason why the human race has not achieved, and never will achieve, its full potential, that word would be "meetings."

—Dave Barry

Long story, short. Keep meetings lean by assigning time limits and moderators to get you out of the conference room and back into the game.

Defeat the Villains of Meetings

Meetings are a waste of time. Just ask any CEO.

According to the study "What Do CEOs Do?" by economists from Harvard Business School and the London School of Economics, "CEOs spend most of their time (85 percent) with other people. Meetings take up 60 percent of the working hours, and the remaining 25 percent is comprised of phone calls, conference calls, and public events."[1]

Some organizations have a culture that forces employees to spend their entire day in meetings. They have to complete any work they generate before or after these 9-to-5 marathons, or even on the weekends.

When you're in a meeting, you're not working. You're stuck in a conference room, and all your productivity has screeched to a halt.

But how can brevity break the bonds of wasteful meetings?

In this chapter, we will explore ways to make meetings less painful and more productive. Let's look at a few easy targets we can hit to make a dent:

1. *Time*: Reduce the amount we allocate for meetings. Too often, it's predictable and indiscriminate. (Why an hour? Wouldn't half an hour be enough?)

2. *Type*: Alter the basic format. Frequently, we're holding a meeting wrong for the objective. (Why are people sitting if they could be standing? Where is the agenda? Why not a round table or *no* table at all?)

3. *Tyrants*: Take down the people that run, rule, and ruin meetings. (Why is the same person always talking? Do you really need a presenter?)

People get stuck in bad meeting habits and mired in the predictable and mundane. Regardless of the meeting type, brevity needs a seat at the table, forcing people to get to the point quickly and accomplish more in less time.

Meeting Villain #1: Time

Meetings often waste time because people schedule *too much* time for them. Trim your agenda to what's necessary.

If you need to talk about one item for only 7 minutes, don't allocate 10. It's like your mother always said: Don't put more on your plate than you can eat. Although 3 extra minutes might not seem like much, this habit will accumulate hours of lost time. Giving yourself more than you need is like throwing valuable minutes down the garbage chute.

Imagine an hour-long staff meeting shrunk to 30 minutes. What if every meeting started and ended on time? Consider meetings that could have flexible lengths that fit your exact needs, such as a 21-minute or 14-minute meeting.

Another enemy of efficiency is lack of preparation and purpose. People come to meetings without being ready or having a clear understanding of the meeting's objective. Are you there to make a decision or to have a discussion? You can lose more than 10 minutes just trying to decipher *why* you are there.

To tackle this villain, consider giving people the first 5 minutes of each meeting to prepare and organize their points quietly. State the purpose up front and let them take this time to review what they need. This will prevent those who come unprepared from wasting even more time rambling to cover their disorganization.

The additional silence up front might seem strange at first, but it will set a nonnegotiable standard for preparing and having a clear point.

Meeting Villain #2: Type

There is very little creativity when it comes to meeting design. From the agenda to the way the room is set up, organizers often end up repeating old, tired habits, citing the excuse, "That's the way we do it around here." But to get more done, you need to find innovative ways for attendees to interact.

Design meetings to be succinct and to succeed. One approach is to stand in huddle formation to indicate you won't be there for long. It's a novel method that removes the comfort of the common meeting. Having everyone stand makes the gathering feel more like a timeout and less like a meeting that's going to go long. This will create a stronger sense of urgency and purpose for everyone. You get to the point faster. People will know how to act.

Another effective way to change up meeting design is eliminating PowerPoint altogether. Speakers can use video, illustrations, or even have their comments drawn in real time by meeting illustrators. If you use a whiteboard to have people express their thoughts, you'll see comments come to life visually—rather than being bored to death slide by slide. Immediate and lasting connections form when verbal and visual realities come together at once.

Meeting Villain #3: Tyrants

A widespread brevity killer in meetings is the *tyrant*—the dominant voice that stifles the chance for conversation. This Type A personality does most of the talking because of rank, personality, or position in the company.

Here are three polite ways to offset the overbearing voice:

- *Assign active listeners.* Debunk tyrants by appointing someone we call an active listener to moderate a more balanced meeting.

  This role is strict: The active listener doesn't speak right away but takes notes and listens for a common thread. His or her job is to keep the meeting short and succinct and to provide a final summary. When a dominant voice threatens to derail or distract the purpose of the meeting, the active listener is obligated to step in.

  I've been in meetings in which the most senior leader took on this role; in others, it was democratically assigned to a different person every time. In each case, taking on that role sends the message that dominant voices aren't welcome.

- *"Stick" to one speaker at a time.* Another approach is to use a talking stick. We have one in my house; it's just a wooden spatula, but with such a large family, my kids all talk over each other at the dinner table, and we needed a way to keep conversations fair. Whoever has the spatula can speak while everyone else must listen. It is a prized possession, a great teaching tool, and funny to see in action.

[brief] **BITS**

If you say everything, they'll hear nothing.

⌈ IT'S AN ⌉
⌊ AMBUSH! ⌋

If you aren't disciplined to remove unnecessary information, then nothing will stick. If people are getting interrupted 50 times a day, checking their smartphone every few minutes, and having to attend nonstop meetings, they'll likely miss every third word you say—unless you beat them to it and first cut out the fluff.

- *Designate time slots.* Finally, drown out dominant speakers by giving everyone a limited time to talk. Make it a rule that only one person can comment on an idea so that you don't have a pile-on effect. You have one-degree commentary and you move on.

    There's a number of other creative ways to run meetings. For more ways, check out books such as *Death by Meeting: A Leadership Fable … About Solving the Most Painful Problem in Business* (Lencioni, 2004), *The Manager's Guide to Effective Meetings* (Streibel, 2002), and *Boring Meetings Suck: Get More Out of Your Meetings, or Get Out of More Meetings* (Petz, 2011).

Change the Format and Tone—Make It a Conversation

After serving as Commander General of the 82nd Airborne Division, General William B. Caldwell IV was chosen to go to Baghdad to work for Multinational Force Iraq as the Strategic Communications Director. Basically, Caldwell was selected to serve as the chief media spokesperson. Publicly, things were not going well in Iraq at the time. So he was handpicked to improve the communication effort in the area during these challenging times.

Gen. Caldwell's predecessor liked to brief the media from behind the podium. He gave a very structured speech every week, like a lecture—a series of prepared, formal, and one-way comments, with limited time for questions and answers.

But Gen. Caldwell, who was new at the media game, wasn't comfortable standing in front of the room and delivering a news sermon. He found it didn't work for him—or the people listening. So he decided to bring in an executive table on his second or third media update and place it in the middle of the room. He removed the podium and rows with a new floor layout. He sat right at the table with the news media—like CNN, the *New York Times*, and BBC—all around, and simply engaged them in a conversation about what was going on inside Iraq.

Gen. Caldwell's approach caught the media off guard. They weren't sure what to make of it. But Gen. Caldwell was very conscientious of making sure that they all knew that he wasn't going to waste their time. He was aware that the meeting was as much for them to gather information as it was for him to tell the story.

Gen. Caldwell prepared for the briefing over the course of each week. He used a Narrative Map to (at least try to) limit the reporters to 30 or 45 minutes. He would walk into a room, say hello, and then say, "I've got about 10 minutes of information to talk to you about—and then we can take questions for another 15 minutes or so."

The media walked out with a better understanding of Gen. Caldwell's message. Instead of just standing up and doing a typical Army briefing with slides, charts, and pictures, the key objective for him was to make it *conversational*. The new setting and approach ensured that everybody felt comfortable in the room and felt confident that they were getting their questions answered.

Gen. Caldwell is also a notorious note taker. He would take notes and write down names while engaging in conversation with the news media. Then if a subject came up during the week, he could call and directly speak to the person who'd asked about it.

He shifted the narrative from an official tone about the affairs in Iraq to a more open, conversational one. Gen. Caldwell formatted the setting and delivery so it felt dramatically different. His bold approach helped change the playing field.

Put BRIEF Back into a Briefing

Military briefings are not known for being clear, concise, or compelling; in fact, far from it. They are typically painful PowerPoint presentations filled with bullets and bad charts, low-resolution images, and poorly formatted graphs.

Jordan, a young military officer who works for U.S. Special Operations Command, took a different tack and strayed away from the standard approach. And he succeeded.

He and his troop had been working for several months on a CONOP, or concept of operations plan, to be submitted to a four-star general for final approval. "Once he approves the plan, we can execute it," he said. "It's a big decision point for us. All of us had been working on this for months with about 25 people touching it."

The amount of time it took to plan, vet, and revise the document was significant. The PowerPoint ballooned to 30 to 40 pages as they briefed it to various agency and Department of Defense stakeholders.

"As you send it up the chain (of command) and all the different staffs and commands have a chop at it, everyone has input," Jordan said. "[So] we wanted to get all the slides right."

But they only had 30 minutes to brief the commander. So they really had to cut the slide count down.

"We wanted to keep it short: 8 to 10 slides," Jordan recalls. Given the amount of trimming, everyone was fairly attached to the final set.

The final briefing, however, took an odd turn. More than a dozen people were in the briefing—Intel, Operations, and staff officers, as well as his unit commander and guys from his troop. And Jordan was the lead briefer. "A lot of stars," he explains. Clearly, the stakes were high.

About 10 minutes before the briefing started, one of the four-star's staff officers decided to pull Jordan aside to give him some pointed advice.

"All the four-star really cares about is to look into your eyes and know that you know what you're talking about. So don't really worry about the slides; just tell him the plan," he cautioned Jordan.

A moment of truth: Should he brief with the slides, as he had planned all along, or simply have a conversation?

"I decided to give his advice a shot," says Jordan. "I felt the slides were my safety net. If I got uncomfortable with the way things were going, I could always fall back into them."

Even though there was some hesitancy to abandon the slide deck, especially with his unit commander there, Jordan felt that he'd received dependable advice from the staff officer. He explained, "This guy knows what he's talking about. He knows the four-star better than I do." And so he decided to take his advice.

Everyone walked in the room, sat down with paper copies, and waited for the commander to enter. Because he was running late, they'd need to complete the briefing in even less time than they'd originally assumed. After apologizing for his lateness, the commander asked for everyone to be introduced—and Jordan got the nod to begin.

As Jordan tells it, "At that point, it's sink or swim. I've spent months and I know the plan, so I talked through essentially what we wanted to do in commonsense terms. There's only one point where I referred him to a picture."

"Because I'm sitting close and talking to him, he was very engaged. It was very much like he and I were having a conversation. He asked questions as we went through. Then at the end he turned to each of his staff officers and got their input."

"And then, in a very jovial fashion, he says, 'Hey, Jordan, do you think this is a good idea?' And, of course, I said yes and everyone laughed. He said 'approved.'"

When you are well prepared and have developed a plan that you're ready to present, remember that people prefer a conversation and value your clarity and confidence. Jordan is now convinced that using a PowerPoint would have been a huge mistake. As he explains, "The commander was coming straight from a meeting. He's got 10 to 12 sessions in a given day where he receives a staggering amount of information. If I'm trying to talk to him and he's trying to read all this text and digest all these pictures on a slide, it would have been a very different brief. More likely, it would have been, 'Sounds great. I'll get back to you; let me talk to my staff.' I don't think we would have been as likely to get a decision right then and there."

Afterward, a lot of people—including his unit commander—commented on the level of rapport he built with the commander. One even commented that he "treated you like his son."

Since that briefing, Jordan has given a lot of thought to this bold approach and says he's realized that "in most cases, the slides are less for the decision maker and more for the staff and subordinate commanders on the way up. Everyone wants to protect the decision maker. The slides are less valuable for the actual briefing."

Long story, short. Keep meetings lean by assigning time limits and moderators to get you out of the conference room and back into the game:

- Is there a regular meeting in your organization at which you can employ the stand-up or the round table model? Try it once, and see how it changes things.

- Ask the key questions before you start the huddle: who, what, when, where, why, and how? Once you've hit those points, you'll be sure to head in the same direction.

- Set a clear time limit and share that with everyone. Designate an active listener to make sure the meeting ends on schedule.

- Let each person know ahead of time how long he or she will have and which points each person will be responsible for covering. Be prepared to abandon the PowerPoint and just have a conversation; if you're well prepared, everyone will welcome it.

12 Leaving a Smaller Digital Imprint

I have only made this letter longer because I have not had the time to make it shorter.

—Blaise Pascal

Long story, short. Make social media posts and e-mails that capture and respect a busy executive's time.

The Digital Flood

It's official: we're all wired.

A 2013 study on Internet trends by Mary Meeker and Liang Yu reports that people check their smartphones an average of 150 times a day.[1]

Everyone's glued to his or her electronic devices—in airports; at the office; walking between meetings; before, during, and after work; even sneaking it at home. We're also hooked to our smartphones, tablets, and e-mail.

A July 2012 McKinsey Global Institute report says managing e-mail takes 28 percent of the average worker's time. You spend a large chunk of your time just keeping up with the constant flow of messages coming in throughout the course of the day.[2]

In the midst of this massive data dump, people check their Twitter feeds nonstop, tantalized by the appetizing 140-character limit. Professionals scan their LinkedIn status updates to gauge who is coming and going and what business news they need to share. Addicted to our devices, we add tons of content that mostly gets lost in the rising flood.

So, what are the do's and don'ts of brevity in the digital age?

You need to be economical with every word, or you'll be chalked up as just another source of white noise. The last thing people want to read are paragraph-long status updates. Nothing annoys a Facebook user more than having to click "Continue Reading" on a rambling post that doesn't ever come to a definitive point. Social media faux pas such as these will significantly reduce your number of followers. And if you don't practice brevity in social media, you might as well be talking to yourself.

You must not only struggle to fit your message into a digestible length within this arena, but also fight against the sheer *frequency* of messages. You're doubtlessly connected to people who are serial online updaters, begging for constant attention, yet unwittingly screaming to be passed over. Don't imitate their bad habits. These people clearly don't practice any self-control and abuse their new-found online freedom to share whatever comes to mind. Do I really need to know when they missed a flight connection or that they just ate a delicious ham sandwich?

Clearly, this new, long-winded abuse of power can quickly be career limiting—because these individuals are training the world to tune them out. They may have good intentions, but they aren't sensitive to being brief. They fail to appreciate that everything they post, share, or send must be valuable, pertinent, and to the point.

Telling always beats selling

▶ Ditch the sales pitch. It's just a conversation.

There are people of the other extreme who set the bar very high. Everything they publish is worth reading. Their e-mails, updates, and e-newsletters reflect a mastery of relevance and restraint.

If you're like me, you subscribe to many newsletters until your inbox is flooded with them every day. You don't have time to read them all, so you either delay reading them or delete them.

What influences your decision about what to read? There are those select few that you absolutely must look at every week; their attractiveness is no accident. They stand apart because they speak in headlines and give you only what is relevant, short, and to the point. It's economical, and it's powerful.

Busy executives make quick judgments about what they want to read. Therefore, the way you communicate digitally must fit on a cracker.

Take, for instance, e-mail. One executive I know keeps his messages brief by writing all of his e-mails on his smartphone and limiting each message to what will fit on a little screen without scrolling. He knows he'll ramble on and on if he writes his e-mails on his laptop. "My boss reads e-mail on the run; that's why I keep it short," he admits.

In this chapter we will look at successes of leaving a smaller digital imprint to make a much bigger impression.

BRIEF Hall of Fame: Verne Harnish

Verne Harnish is a master of brevity.

He is the "Growth Guy" columnist for *Fortune Magazine* and the epitome of BRIEF. As the founder of the Entrepreneurs' Organization and CEO of the global executive education and coaching company Gazelles, Harnish targets C-level executives by headlining and honing every e-mail, newsletter, and post. Every message he sends obviously indicates his preparation in making it clear and concise. It's unmistakable; you see his discipline in action in every correspondence.

- *Catchy headline*: There's always a strong attention-grabber in bold.
- *Predictable length*: The paragraphs are never more than a few sentences.
- *Tightly written*: He's never wordy and *always* relevant.
- *Time saving*: There are often direct references to saving you time, from "take 3 minutes to read this whitepaper" to encouraging growth leaders to huddle for 15 minutes a day.

Not a moment is wasted when Verne's readers follow up on his recommendations. It's apparent that he cares about and respects their time. Within each of his newsletter's sections, Verne executes a balanced structure between what information his readers need to know and the "so what" behind it.

And his strategy makes a *huge difference*. Not only does he give me primary resources to back up the headlines, but he always tells me why it's important.

Even his columns adhere to the rules of brevity. His *Fortune* column has only five tips, every time. As he explains, "I get 75 words for each tip, and it is painful to try to figure out how you're going to make something credible and useful enough in 75 words." But "It's been a good discipline. And it was out of necessity. It's the nature of the market."

"These are CEOs and executives of growth companies. By nature, they're a tough group to reach. They are just time crunched."

Harnish thinks like a journalist when he carefully crafts catchy headlines to outline his newsletters. Social media might be instant, but it takes time to reduce your ideas to as few words as possible.

"I know I spend as much or more time trying to figure out what the headlines are than what I write next," he said. "I think writing headlines is a discipline every leader needs to adopt."

Verne does this so that busy executives can scan his newsletters literally in 30 seconds and determine whether there's anything useful. And all of the sections catch their attention; that's why he has such a loyal following.

"I let them know specifically how long it's going to take for them to dig in to something if they want to, so they can make decisions to do it now or later," he said. Harnish emphasizes that all executives need to practice communicating briefly.

"You state it simply. Doesn't mean it's *simple*, but you do it so that the world gets it and can understand it."

When it comes to getting your message heard, it's best to use as few powerful words as possible.

Be brief in explaining what you do, so that your audience can compartmentalize and get your message.

From Social Media to Venture Capital

There's power in a simple anecdote shared online. By keeping her story and products simple enough to share, develop, and sell online, Brandi Temple won $20 million in venture capital for her children's clothing company, Lolly Wolly Doodle (LWD).

According to Temple, LWD has become a master innovator at social commerce because her company's story is so simple and powerful. By harnessing social media to showcase its products,

Lolly Wolly Doodle does 60 percent of its sales through Facebook and the remainder through its website.

"When things started taking off, I used customers as my sounding board. I interacted daily on [our] Facebook page, sharing my story and designing clothes based on customer feedback," she said. "In turn, the customers became evangelists for the brand. Much of Lolly Wolly Doodle's current success can be attributed to the relationship we have with our loyal fans."

Each of the brand's Facebook posts is only about 30 words; it describes the product, price, and available sizes, with a picture attached. Within minutes of each post, followers comment to request the sizes and colors they want. And this formula works. When I spoke to Temple during the summer of 2013, LWD had more than 605,000 Facebook fans.

"I couldn't find outfits I liked for my two daughters, so I just started making clothing for my kids out of necessity," she said. "I started sewing and then I made too much and thought of putting the extras out there on eBay and then Facebook. It came naturally."

LWD's manufacturing model attracted investors because it responded immediately and exclusively to customer's needs.

"We produce only what our customers order, and we're always tweaking designs based on what they say they want to see," Temple said.

The only way that Temple could have accomplished such a reactive model was by using the instantaneous advantage of social media.

"The best way I can experience the joy of Lolly Wolly Doodle is to share our clothing, and let our community share their stories with us," she said.

The feedback process that drove venture capital to Temple's door wasn't complicated. Customers gave short reviews online; Temple listened and responded accordingly. A simple, short story of success that was shared online by loyal fans propelled her business.

Social media is an arena where masters of brevity thrive. Your content can reach an unlimited audience; so make sure it is finely tuned to meet customers' expectations of brevity.

Social Media Squeeze

If you struggle to get your thoughts down to a Twitter-tight 140-character limit, listen closely. According to Adam Brown, corporate social media pioneer at such leading brands as Coca-Cola, Dell, and Salesforce.com, the ideal level of engagement is even *lower*.

"Actually, the most effective social media posts are around 80 characters," says Brown. "The most engaging from a branding and marketing standpoint are that (amount) or shorter. They are twice as effective as those at 140."

So it's time to learn to sharpen your tongue.

According to Brown, social media's evolution can be characterized by a push for brevity. From blogs and microblogs to Twitter, Instagram, and beyond, there has been a growing emphasis to make communication easier and shorter to produce and share content online. But the level of energy and commitment needed to create quality social media cannot be ignored.

"There are a lot of people who have Facebook and Twitter fatigue nowadays," says Brown. "It's too much effort. Everyone began to realize 'This is a lot of work; there's only so many hours and minutes a day I can allocate to this.'"

Brown asserts that there are new and traditional skills that we all need to hone to stand out online.

"Social media that has a visual component is about five times more engaging than text," he states. "The next evolution of social media is going to be that you don't have to participate in the creation of the content that appears. You'll wear something around your neck that takes a picture every minute or two and automatically checks you in wherever you go and knows your friends are surrounding you. It becomes something passive." For the moment, however, being active means being *succinct*.

Ironically, Brown asserts, our education is somewhat at fault for our verbosity. The classic educational approach is to have students write to achieve a minimum word limit, for instance, an 800-word essay. To win mindshare in social media, however, is to do the exact opposite.

"It's fundamentally *against* the way we have been trained to write," he says. But nowadays, to succeed means to condense.

"Most people consume social media on their mobile devices. I call it the 'brand in the hand.' It's very likely the person is on the move—on the subway, waiting to pick up their kids," Brown says. "The bottom line is: they're doing something else. So you've got to get those nuggets of wisdom, or conversation, or storytelling briefer and more succinct."

Long story, short. Make social media posts and e-mails that capture and respect a busy executive's time:

- How can you make your organization's e-mail newsletters or social media posts more to the point?

- Pretend you're the reader. What headline or image would grab your attention and make you read more?

- How can your customers help you with your digital imprint? Let them tell you briefly what they want from you, and they will be able to respond instantly. Allow them to share snippets of success online.

13 Presenting a Briefer Case

The secret of a good sermon is to have a good beginning and a good ending, and to have the two as close together as possible.

—George Burns

Long story, short. See how a presentation as succinct as a general's brief and svelte as a TED Talk can respect an audience and catch its attention.

Practicing What You Preach

The thought of hearing a long sermon probably doesn't thrill you.

Imagine that you are sitting in a church and the preacher stands up at the podium and begins his remarks. Chances are, you're thinking something like, "How long is this going to last? Is it going to mean anything to me? Will it be different from all the speeches I've heard before?"

Are you enthused? Or dreading that he might go on forever?

And when your fears become a reality, and the remarks have gone over an hour with no end in sight, do you think, "Why does praying feel so painful?"

So then why do the same thing to your captive audience when it's time for *you* to give a presentation? Perhaps it's out of vengeance, but what makes everyone think that bigger is better when it comes to speeches?

If the mere mention of the word *presentations* immediately triggers what your PowerPoint is going to include, then you need to think again. Your mind should instead leap to your audience's needs and wants. Respect them.

However, few executives feel comfortable without the crutch of their slides when left standing alone in front of a room of people. Unfortunately, the people in your audience don't care. They have even more on their minds and will check out mentally or grab their smartphones or tablets if you don't get to the point.

Thankfully, we are seeing some relief on the horizon. New presentation formats from conferences like TED limit the presenters to no more than 18 minutes and dictate strict presenter guidelines.

In this chapter, experienced presenters will share their advice on effective communication in front of a desperate, distracted audience.

The Discipline of Brevity

Brigadier General Rich Gross of the U.S. Army serves as legal counsel to the Chairman of the Joint Chiefs of Staff. In other words, he advises the highest-ranking military staff officer in the United States. Gross is a remarkable man for many reasons, but he's also a rarity: he's a lawyer that's brief. And as he himself admits, "Lawyer's briefs are never brief."

The lives of those in the military are exponentially busier than those of most civilians. Gross is hyperaware that his updates need to fit into the Chairman of the Joint Chief of Staff's tight schedule.

"National security problems are more complex and comprehensive," Gross said. "And you have to combine that with the busy lives, the complex situations we face—then the onslaught of information, the 24-hour news cycle, the constant Blackberry, and cell phones and smartphones that are with us all of the time."

Even though Gross deals with some of the most important and complicated national security legal problems, he is able to cut his updates to a page or less.

"We tend to think that complex issues can't be brief," he said. "But you have to realize how busy people are, and how much they have to retain about hundreds of issues at any given time. I constantly remind myself, 'If I can say it in one page, that's better than two. If half a page will do it, that's better than one.'"

Gross also teaches at the University of Virginia Law School and Georgetown Law School. He cited the inefficient tendency lawyers have to include everything plus the kitchen sink when presenting a problem or a case.

"They make every possible argument they can to a court, hoping that one will stick," he said. "One of the techniques that I teach and have always used in my own writing is 'bottom line upfront.' There's nothing worse than a memo or a legal opinion from a lawyer that you have to read down to their signature block to figure out what the recommendation is."

Gross lets readers of all his e-mails and documents know exactly what the topic is *before* they finish the first paragraph.

"Nobody gets past that first paragraph or that opening first minute or two of a briefing without having already ingrained in their minds where I'm going and what I need from them," he said. "If you don't tell them that up front and just start giving them the background details, then they're not listening actively."

─── [brief] BASICS ───

START WITH WHY:
START DEFINING THE PROBLEM

"Why?" is a very powerful question that defines the problem your company is trying to solve.

Think about how you'd describe an object like a chair. You immediately list off a series of attributes: four legs, a seat, a backrest, and wood or metal construction. For a business, the description might include history, products, location, and financials.

But you probably won't explain **why** there are chairs or why your business exists.

In his book *Start with Why*, author Simon Sinek asserts that most organizations fail completely to explain why and rather elect to talk extensively about **other details,** such as how, where, how much, and when. By omitting the why, they leave us **lost** in the weeds (e.g., You were founded in 1968. But why is that important?)

To be effective and efficient, you need to get at the **essence.** For instance, the reason you have a chair is to provide relief when you get tired of standing. The core point of your business really means **defining the problem.** By telling us why, everything you say from that point on is a logical way to **resolve** that pressing problem (e.g., now I understand why your history matters so much).

Implications:

▶ **Answer the pressing question first.** People are most satisfied when they're given a clear reason why up front.

▶ **Eliminate confusion.** As you can dig down into the details, people can stay focused and see how it all fits together.

▶ **Uncover the core problem.** You can get to the point quickly because the why isolates and defines the central issue.

He also pointed out that people usually make the mistake of assuming that everyone is on the same page when jumping into a topic or discussion. "We think everybody has the same experience and background that we do," he explains.

If you don't check to make sure everyone is up to date, some of your audience members might spend the majority of your presentation trying to orient themselves on the topic.

To prevent losing his audience before he even begins, Gross tries to put himself in the mind of his client or the audience.

"People say, 'Know your audience.' But you not only have to know them; you have to speak their *language*."

According to Gross, being brief and effective takes fearless, militant discipline. Cast out the following excuses for untrained presentation skills.

1. *You're afraid of losing your audience.* If people think they're losing the audience, losing the argument, or not making the case that they need to make, they ramble. Prepare your presentation to be as convincing as possible and make sure everyone is caught up from the beginning. If you've done your homework properly, your point will drive itself home.

2. *You're devoted to the slides, not the content.* Gross prefers avoiding PowerPoint. Instead, memorize your *three key points* and know the material backward and forward. This frees you from having to constantly glance back at a slide.

3. *You're afraid of missing the point.* There's no reason to be anxious that you won't get all of the information out in a learning environment. As long as you reach your main argument, no one will be any wiser if you skip some details, especially if you don't have PowerPoint slides to give you away.

4. *You're passionate about the topic.* Passionate presenters want the audience to feel the same way they do. But being

long-winded won't help you get there. Strong, compelling, well-summarized ideas will.

5. *You don't have time to make an outline.* This is never the case; there is always time to make an outline. Either in your head or on a napkin, decide on your presentation's purpose, three key words, and the conclusion of your presentation. This is a crucial precursor for any successful presentation.

If a U.S. Army general can simplify and summarize the military's complex legal points into a page or less, you have no excuse not to be brief. It may be challenging—but do the legwork beforehand to make your ideas as succinct and compact as possible.

Putting the Power Back in PowerPoint

Bernardo Valenzuela, vice president of the Chicago transportation equipment manufacturer Navistar, presented to his senior leaders about the company's international expansion—in just seven slides.

Valenzuela noticed that some of the leaders who presented before him took hours to build their presentations, so he decided to do something different. "It was simple and logical, and it made a lot of sense to them," he said. "I used the first three slides to discuss our current situation, give some background information, and present our opportunity. "The last slide caught their attention because it showed the leaders how much profit we could be making."

Valenzuela's presentation was so successful that the leaders later approached him for an encore.

"They called me that night and asked if I could do the presentation again," he said.

Not only did Valenzuela distill his message to a half-dozen slides, he also structured his presentation to lead up to the final action item: the potential profit. Most executives are usually forced to listen to disorganized, lengthy, and inconclusive presentations. No wonder Valenzuela's higher-ups were desperate to have him speak again.

Brevity saved the day in Valenzuela's case, and demonstrated his value and objectivity to the top leaders of his company. He got their attention and, more importantly, their support.

Training as a TED Talk

TED is a set of global conferences focused on technology, entertainment, and design. As a part of the Sapling Foundation, TED presentations showcase videos of the best, most inspiring ideas in 18 minutes or less.

TED speakers and employees always use plain, short words; they know that being brief honors their audience's time and attention. Their mission is simple—"ideas worth sharing." And while your idea might be worthy, it's the sharing part that gets tricky.

Emily McManus has been the editor of TED's website since January 2007. To represent the brand's philosophy online, McManus teaches her staff to whittle their content down to its essence, much as a TED speaker does.

"The idea of staying brief [and] staying current really requires a lot of effort up front," McManus said. She explains that you need to invest time in honing your presentation's structure and content. It's all about timing the material to guide the audience through the necessary premises.

"By 5 minutes in, you need to get into the middle arc of your story," McManus said. "The best thing you can do if you're trying to compress is *not* try to tell the entire story of your entire field in 15 minutes. [Rather, you want to] give an intriguing single story."

Once the people in the audience have been prepped with the right background information, give them the final message, take a bow, and then take a seat.

"The best speakers are the ones whose story has a beginning, a middle, and an end, but starts in the middle," McManus said. "People who talk about very specialized subjects need the ability to give an overview of a field in a few minutes. They lay out some of the hard problems and then focus on one specific aspect of that problem."

In a particularly memorable TED Talk, Elizabeth Gilbert tells her story about what is at play with creative genius. She muses about what makes people capable of breakthrough insights, focusing on her own unexpected publishing success and where it all comes from to produce a runaway idea (http://www.ted.com/talks/elizabeth_gilbert_on_genius.html).

Speaking to such a large audience is stressful, but putting in the proper work beforehand can help you capture your listeners with brevity. In addition, McManus recommends giving your text to people to review. They'll likely catch the lapses in brevity you may have missed.

[brief] **BITS**

The less you say, the more likely you'll be heard.

$\begin{bmatrix} \text{BITE THE} \\ \text{BULLET!} \end{bmatrix}$

A friend of mine once described his father in these terms: "My dad didn't talk much when we were growing up, but when he said something, everybody paid attention. You didn't miss what he had to say." If we are careful, controlled, and conscious of the moment, we can say little and have people hear a lot.

"One of the techniques that I teach my staff members is to look for the verb. If they're using a form of 'to be,' you're probably missing a punchier, sexier, shorter verb."

You can use official TED standards to make your presentation TED Talk-worthy. They state verbatim that "long talks, podiums and readings are discouraged" and maintain that a speaker should be able to write the idea in "one or two sentences."

If you can't meet that challenge, then it's time to go back to the drawing board. For your next PowerPoint presentation, cut the number of slides you use in half. Then do it again. And again.

Even better, as we discussed in the previous chapter: present *without* slides.

Check out www.TED.com. Watch a few of the most popular talks. Notice how the speakers use simple, clear, and brief language.

If people in your audience want or need more information, they'll come to you. As long as you value their time, they will see you as a treasured, objective source of information.

Long story, short. See how a presentation as succinct as a general's brief and svelte as a TED Talk can respect an audience and catch its attention.

14 Trimming Your Sales (Pitch)

It is my ambition to say in 10 sentences what others say in a whole book.

—Friedrich Nietzsche

Long story, short. Buyers and sellers will benefit from shorter pitches that are on target.

Shut Up and Sell

Everyone is in the business of buying and selling ideas. And whatever side of the table you've sat on—either as the seller or buyer—you've seen what both great *and* terrible look like when it comes to brevity.

Early in my career, my first sales manager wisely cautioned his recruits: "Don't talk through the close—shut up and sell." It was meant as a bold reminder of brevity. Although it's tempting to think that talking more means you're smarter, more prepared, and more convincing, the opposite is true.

Everyone needs to keep answers short.

I've seen so many train wrecks in this arena: salespeople who get overexcited, overenthusiastic, overcaffeinated, and overexplanatory. It'd be better for them to be more conversational and ask more questions. The role of active listening is absolutely vital, yet rarely practiced.

Regardless of which end you're on, people should feel balance, respect, and restraint throughout the buying and selling process.

───────────────────────────── [brief] **BITS** ───

Tell; don't sell.

People would much rather hear a story than endure a sales pitch. According to Kendall Haven, author of *Story Proof*, "People are eager for stories. Not dissertations. Not lectures. Not informative essays." Storytelling is a lost art that needs urgent rediscovery. Persuasion is an art too, but storytelling always satisfies, whereas selling leaves people cold.

Billboard on a Bumper Sticker

Kristi Faulkner is the president and founder of Womenkind, a small New York City advertising agency that was featured on the AMC network's reality show *The Pitch* in 2012. Her team battled for an account and Faulkner said the brevity of the pitch was a key consideration to determine the winner.

She's well aware that in the advertising world, it's cut or be cut.

"I think that ideas in particular have to be extremely brief. Three words are better than four, or four words are better than six," she said. "When you're trying to get an idea across to someone else, it should be crystal clear and easy to communicate."

Faulkner explains that having a distilled idea is more likely to impact and inspire a potential client during a pitch.

"You'd think that the more you throw at them, the better chances you have of selling something, but it's actually not the case," she said. "You're going to have a better chance by throwing *one* ball at one target."

People react immediately when Faulkner is pitching a singular idea that sticks. "They jump in, and they always build on it," she describes.

However, it can be difficult to get everybody on the same page about the core idea.

"You need to get it down to as few words as possible," Faulkner says. "That's fewer opportunities for people to become confused or to go off on tangents. Fewer words lead to greater clarity."

Faulkner cited successful slogans like Volkswagen's campaign in the 1960s: "Think Small," and even the Declaration of Independence.

"You have to reduce your message to its simplest version," she said. "It should be able to fit on a billboard or a bumper sticker."

Faulkner continues, "A lack of confidence and security usually make people add those two or three extra words. If you think the idea needs an explanation, then it's not a good idea yet," she said. "But that's the work of writing. Writing is about rewriting. You keep rewriting, and it's boring—and that's the truth."

Even though she's a successful creative leader and entrepreneur, Faulkner admits that she sometimes has trouble describing her own firm.

"It's difficult, and I think that this is where every company has a challenge," she admitted.

But after some work, Faulkner whittled down Womenkind's tagline to "Marketing communications that respect the economic power of women."

"We want to tell all the chapters and all the verses, but it's not really that memorable or compelling," she said.

Her agency's narrative, in fact, starts with the opportunity to recognize women. Her company is successful because it focuses on resolving this issue and respecting their economic power.

Faulkner's simple pitch helps Womenkind stand apart. Your campaign should be just as tight and catchy.

Time to Be Convincing and Concise

Elie Maalouf is an experienced business executive and the former head of global food and beverage concessions provider HMSHost. He has had many opportunities over the course of his career to present to various boards of directors and make high-level sales presentations.

Maalouf knows that even if you have all the right experience and recommendations, you still need to convince the board during your presentation. He says that those critical moments are the time to tailor your material to the audience.

"The key to brevity in the boardroom is to always start by asking, what does the board *already* know?" Maalouf said. "You really must have a good feeling for what the shared platform of information is. It's vital to first understand that common ground."

This is also true for sales presentations. Don't waste time introducing yourself to clients who already have access to basic information. It's your job to *convince* them why your recommendation should merit their support. Sharing only new and meaningful information will transform your presentation into a conversation.

┌─ [brief] BASICS ──────────────────────────────┐

ELEVATOR SPEECH:
MASTERING WHY, WHAT, AND SO WHAT

A perfected elevator speech allows you to convey your company's message in a short sound byte that inspires and sticks.

At one major university job fair, my company, Sheffield, was the smallest among the Fortune 500 firms in attendance. However, we had the longest line of people waiting to speak with us throughout the day.

The way we **simply and quickly** explained the story of our growing business—our elevator speech—created instant appeal. People wanted to hear our David versus Goliath tale of how we were taking down big agencies with our nimble focus on **narratives.** They were intrigued to hear how we were creating fulfilling career opportunities for liberal arts majors.

At the end of the day, the event coordinator was astonished at the number of people who came to speak with us. "What were you telling them?" I gave her my **elevator speech**. Forty-five seconds later she just smiled. "You know many of the recruiters here, especially from the big firms, can't clearly explain what their companies do the way you just did."

Implications:

► **Keep the story short.** Create instant interest and a lasting impression.

► **Initiate and invite a conversation.** You don't want to just grab people's attention; you have to get them involved and talking.

► **Build real interest.** Avoid meaningless monologues, and ensure people feel invited to participate and ask questions.

└──┘

"People spend 50 percent of their time telling you about themselves and about their company's history and products. [But customers] just want to know what's different and what's better," Maalouf explains. "I want to make it a discussion; a monologue shouldn't come until the end."

"Going over traveled ground just dilutes the strength of the punch and the time that you have. I learned to appreciate those people who have studied the circumstances."

Timing is crucial in these situations. As Maalouf explains, "If you don't make an impression that you have something different and valuable in the first 5 or 10 minutes, the chances of the next 20 minutes being of use to you are slim—because people are going to fault that impression very early."

Observe the impact your statements are making by reading the audience's body language. You can tell if the information you're sharing is sinking in, or whether somebody wants to stop and dive in somewhere. Doing what Maalouf calls machine-gunning will always lead to failure.

"Speaking slowly and sensing the mood in the room will give you command of the situation. You'll also be able to stop where you need and to take a question," Maalouf said. "Because when people are festering on a question, they're not hearing the next 10 pages you go through."

You also need to be prepared to condense your pitch at a moment's notice. Recently, while presenting to a CEO in India, Maalouf saw his allotted time shrink from 2 hours to 30 minutes. Don't get caught off guard by unpredictable changes.

"I always assume that I have half the time formally available," he said. "You never know when there's a delay in start, an early finish, or an interruption."

Ditch the PowerPoint slides when stepping into the board-room. You can use them to prepare yourself if that helps you outline your points in your head. But you will seem more prepared and competent if you don't need to lean on the technology.

"I didn't use PowerPoint, but I prepared as if I was. I had my talking points ready and rehearsed them extensively so that I was confident and comfortable going through them in person."

Remember: simple and clear doesn't mean trivial and juvenile. Relieve your audience by delivering the right information clearly and at a pace that doesn't cause people to fall behind.

"Brevity should not be conflated or confused with lack of information," Maalouf warns. "Give your audience brevity and assurance."

Cut to the Customer's Chase

Tom Searcy, an expert in large account sales, recalls cutting off a $20 million pitch from IBM when the presenters failed to answer his questions in a short amount of time. Although both the buyer and the seller felt pretty strongly that IBM would get the deal, the speakers were totally missing the mark.

About 20 minutes into the presentation, Searcy interrupted them and said, "I'm sorry, gentlemen; I will respect your time, and I appreciate your willingness to respect my time. So let me tell you what I need to hear from you today."

Searcy told the presenters specifically which questions he needed answered. They responded by saying, "We're going to get to that, but right now, we have some additional things we want to show you." And they continued to plow through their preset agenda.

Respect people's time

▶ Executives hate wasting time. Your short story will save them.

After going on for another 20 minutes, the speaker still didn't get anywhere close to what Searcy wanted to talk about.

So Searcy interrupted again and said, "I need to be very clear about this: I have *three problems* I'm trying to solve right now, and I believe you can help me solve them. But so far, we haven't spent any time on the three problems that I need to get solved. Can you tell me how you would solve these three problems?"

The speaker said, "Absolutely, we're just about to come to that."

But then 10 more minutes passed and they still hadn't covered any of Searcy's questions. So he said, "Stop. You will answer my three questions now or I will ask you to leave and when you have someone who can answer my questions, send them back."

Within 5 minutes, Searcy ended the meeting. He said, "Send me somebody who can talk to me about my issues."

Some people are stuck on delivering their presentation their way—no matter how detrimental it ends up being to them. IBM's representatives were so disconnected from their audience they destroyed any chance of giving an effective presentation and selling to the customer.

Long story, short. Buyers and sellers will benefit from shorter pitches that are on target.

- Imagine that you're in an office elevator with a potential customer. Can you deliver your pitch in the time it takes to get to your floor? Practice giving it in 2 minutes. Time yourself.

- If you're the seller, listen to your customers instead of focusing only on the pitch. Ask them thoughtful questions to determine their needs—and *listen* to their answers.

- Don't make the mistake of assuming that the more you say, the more prepared you will sound. Busy executives will cut you off or tune you out.

15 Whose Bright Idea Was That Anyway?

One should use common words to say uncommon things.

—Arthur Schopenhauer

Long story, short. The best ideas are explained simply.

Your Big Idea

A number of years ago, my older sister had an inspiration for a device to track items when you lost them. She excitedly revealed her big idea during a holiday gathering. She's not an inventor, but she spent the entire dinner talking about why this device would be a huge hit and how it would make millions of dollars.

When I asked her the (obvious) question about exactly *how* it would work, however, she quickly got flustered and offered up no details.

"It's going to make millions," she said defensively. "Trust me, it will."

Her excitement in that moment reminded me of many executives I've seen who are passionate about a big idea they have—yet are missing key parts of the story. Leaders of organizations will enthusiastically explain a new strategy, mission, set of values, or culture—but because they don't include the important information about *how* it's going to happen, they lose everyone in the process. Then they can't understand why more people don't share their view and cannot get on the same page.

[brief] **BITS**

Brevity is the catalyst of insight and ideas.

When you have a brilliant idea and can clearly and quickly tell a story, word travels fast. Brevity can help make everyone see and feel as you do. Given the sheer amount of obstacles preventing countless good ideas, being clear and concise is one of your best skills.

Brevity plays an essential role in framing and sharing a big idea by making it easy to understand and quick to explain. Brevity keeps an idea's brilliance from getting lost in high-level hype or buried in the minutia.

Let's take a closer look at a variety of examples, ranging from how successful military strategists have used narratives to organize complex mission strategies, to entrepreneurs who struggled to get out of the weeds and elevate their breakthrough idea.

A Mission-Critical Narrative

Colonel Eric Henderson is a forward-thinking military professional who embraces the strategic value of narratives. When he was deployed with the 10th Mountain Division to southern Afghanistan, he decided that he would use storytelling and the BRIEF method to simplify how his group had conceived and explained their strategic plan.

"I wanted to frame the plan as a simple narrative," he said. "People see the world in stories, and I was convinced we could boil down our plan to a storyline—characters and all."

When Henderson returned home a year later, he called me and left me a two-word voicemail: "It works!"

"I was blessed with the best senior communications team I've worked with in 25 years," he told me later. "My public affairs officer was absolutely switched on. As soon as I explained the process of using a narrative to him, he was like, 'This rocks.'"

The commander believed in it. Several of the deputy commanders believed in it. Henderson's boss got it. It was remarkable—since, according to Henderson, that kind of consensus is unusual in the Army.

"We had fairly strong evidence that the story we told was in fact becoming the dominant narrative in the operational area," he said. "Even our enemies were beginning to tell portions of our story our way. People began to explain things in *our* terms, not theirs.

"When you sit down with the brother of a prominent Afghan leader who says, 'Let me explain to you what's *really* going on here'—and you hear him tell the story *you've* been telling all along—that's when you know you've knocked it out of the park," Henderson said.

The heavy lifting for Henderson's communications team involved getting the rest of the company to understand the core narrative: "We tried to understand how the execution of the military operation was in fact an audience participation play—a story."

Henderson explained that even his commander embraced the BRIEF method: "Half the commander's job is just making sure everybody's marching in the same direction at the same speed. If your words are a manifestation of what plans and intentions are, and if your plan really *is* the manifestation of your story, then the commander will tell that story over and over again every time he goes out and talks."

Sometimes his commander had to encapsulate a 40-page campaign plan into a short presentation.

"To carry out the metaphor of the play, you got to be able to break that down to a handbill. And the handbill matters—because if you're clever, it sticks. It will become truth. That was the way we talked to higher headquarters as well."

[brief] **BITS**

[MISSION CRITICAL!]

Only with brevity can clarity generate more clarity.

If what you hear is clear, you're likely to grasp more than what was said. Your imagination builds on the ideas you hear and applies them to your daily problems and strategies. Your listening abilities have the power to amplify simple moments of clarity. Inspiration comes at these moments.

Having a scalable story made it easy for Henderson and his team to incorporate new events and problems into the narrative.

"Without a narrative, at least half of the engagement seems to be reactive," he said. "They say, 'Oh, what are we going to say about it?' And then there's this massive scramble. But using a narrative changes that dynamic. Instead of being rocked on the defensive, it simply becomes evidence of the truth of the story I've been telling from the beginning. The narrative allows you to have a brief expression—an elevator speech with a lot of context."

Henderson continues, "You become better at explaining it. This way, when things happen, the organization's role is not to explain what happened. Rather, it's to explain how that bad thing fits into the story. And the narrative helps you do that: quickly, simply, and in a believable way."

Henderson's success with the BRIEF method during his time in action in Afghanistan demonstrates how a cohesive story can unify and simplify even the most complicated operational strategy. The narrative helped everyone on every level understand, adapt, and execute the plan.

Clear Picture with Radical Focus

Author and entrepreneur Verne Harnish has identified two keys to entrepreneurial success that reflect the value of brevity: clarity and radical focus. He offers Facebook as an example.

"It is this maniacal mission Facebook just came out of, where Zuckerberg woke up December, 2011 and said, 'Oh my God, we missed mobile.' And he totally got the entire company radically focused on that single mission that you could summarize in a single word."

Facebook went mobile in May of the following year.

Harnish explains that "It's difficult for entrepreneurs, because they've got all symptoms of ADHD [attention-deficit/hyperactivity disorder]. It's like a shiny object. The next exciting thing grabs their attention." These distractions cause executives to lose focus of their goal.

"It's what Steve Jobs learned in his wilderness years at Pixar: the power of a team having a *single focus*. Pixar had the luxury and freedom from doing only *Toy Story*. They could put every ounce of their being into that film. That's also why Apple was very disciplined and released one product every two years; not unlike what you do with a movie," Harnish explains.

He goes on, "This radical focus is more important than ever before, mainly because you've got so much more competition. If you're not maniacally dedicated to being the best at something very niche, you're going to get crushed."

Certainly, with that singular vision flows singular expression—and brevity is born.

The Entrepreneur's Dilemma: Mixed Messages

Paul Koziarz and Glen Shimkus struggled when it was time to launch the digital documentation product for realtors they'd developed called Cartavi. Instead of having a simple, clear message, they were telling different stories to investors and customers. Soon, their purpose became muddled.

"Just being an entrepreneur and starting something new is a messy process. You have to develop a story that works with everybody," Koziarz said. "We didn't think that brevity was as important until we realized that people didn't completely understand what Cartavi was."

Unfortunately for Koziarz and Shimkus, their enthusiasm translated only into confusion.

"We wanted to spend hours talking about all the features and functionality, and why it made sense," he said. "But we had a hard time figuring out which story different groups wanted to hear."

I was able to help Koziarz and Shimkus build the story they wanted to tell to their entire audience. We landed on a clear message: they leverage technology to help realtors be more tech savvy and more responsive and to win more business. Their product, which is similar to Dropbox, could advance a realtor's performance because it was simple, mobile, and secure. It took the paperwork out of the transaction and made realtors more effective professionals.

"That's what we saw was resonating, because people were nodding their heads when we talked about the iPad and mobile, and simple user design," Koziarz said. "Those were all things that they appreciated the real value of. In the end, they wanted to be responsive. They didn't care how they were doing it, but Cartavi helped them to be more responsive to clients' needs, even at 12 o'clock at night. They were more professional and there was way more business, because they were taking care of their clients' needs."

Once Cartavi started to develop and refine their concise story over the next year, the team started to notice a difference as the competition grew.

"We saw competitors incorporating pieces of our story into their own products. They were, in some cases, even emulating some of the things we were saying about our composition."

Over the next two years, Cartavi grew by sticking to its core message.

"We didn't have a lot of dollars then, or advertising and marketing blitz," Koziarz said. "But we developed a lot of good relations, one of which was a DocuSign partnership. Now we're seeing larger entities and larger franchises with big real estate brands adopting Cartavi as a viable solution to their needs for document management. It's something we were doing in the first place—but they didn't realize who we were."

"The growth curve has been definitely a hockey stick. It goes straight up. It's been pretty phenomenal."

---[brief] BASICS---

WIFM:
DIAL INTO PAYOFFS AND PUNCH LINES

Whether you're an employee or a customer, one question dominates every proposition: "What's in it for me?"

I learned the term WIFM in Terra Haute, Indiana—not a city with the most robust economy or dynamic tourist destination. I was working with a group from Columbia House, the company made famous by the "for one penny, get 13 8-tracks/Tapes/CDs/DVDs" offer. I was there to help them improve their ability to deliver **updates** as part of a change management initiative driven out of New York.

Over the course of the workshop, I worked closely with mid-level managers and a few dozen of their respective supervisors. After one exercise on how to share news from the corporate office, a woman said to me: "That's fine that we say all that stuff, but the only thing my employees are thinking about the entire time is **'What's in it for me?'** They want to know: 'Am I going to lose my job because of this?'"

It hit me at that moment that being brief means delivering the news—whether it's a beneficial payoff or a painful punch line— **as quickly as possible**. It's what people are waiting to hear.

Implications:

► **Know what motivates your audience.** If you miss this part, you run the risk of losing people—and their attention, respect, time, or trust—right from the start.

► **Skip what doesn't matter.** Know your audience's WIFM. Say fewer things that are purposeful and pointed while discarding what's not essential.

► **Make a conclusive delivery.** Your audience needs to hear you get to the point quickly and decisively as if you were hitting a joke's punch line.

Tailor Your Pitch to Your Investor's Needs

Nina Nashif is the founder and CEO of Healthbox, a platform that helps developing health care businesses prepare their pitches to venture capitalists. She trains executives to deliver exactly what investors need to know in order to make the final decision—and nothing more.

"We've found time and time again that these entrepreneurs begin those conversations by just 'throwing up' their entire business," Nashif said. "They tell the story of how great the business is and what they're solving and what they're doing and everyone who loves it."

But an unfiltered flood of information is not going to impress potential investors. They only want to know why your idea or company deserves *their* support.

"Most entrepreneurs are so passionate about what they're doing that they assume that everyone is going to embrace it in the same way that they do," Nashif said. "They're not thinking, 'How do I explain my business in a way that others will understand?'"

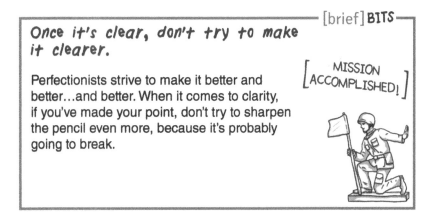

[brief] BITS

Once it's clear, don't try to make it clearer.

Perfectionists strive to make it better and better...and better. When it comes to clarity, if you've made your point, don't try to sharpen the pencil even more, because it's probably going to break.

[MISSION ACCOMPLISHED!]

Nashif explains that whenever an entrepreneur steps into an investor meeting, they need to be prepared to discuss the points their audience needs to hear: "Entrepreneurs end up talking about this really broad landscape instead of guiding the conversation to what an angel investor is going to be more comfortable talking about," she said.

For instance, entrepreneurs need to account for the difference between a venture capitalist and an angel investor. You can't create a blanket presentation for these two distinct audiences. Nashif distinguishes between the two: "Angel investors are interested in helping an entrepreneur test and validate the business and its traction in the market. A venture capitalist wants to know that you've already done that and how you're growing and will become the next $100 million dollar company."

When it comes to interviewing potential new businesses to coach, Nashif makes her decision almost immediately.

"When I'm meeting with an entrepreneur, I know within the first 5 to 10 minutes of their presentation. The first question we start with is, 'Tell us something about your business that we didn't learn. What are you trying to accomplish and what would you want out of working with us?'" she said. "If they start droning all over the place and just talk for an hour, I might still not know what they're doing."

The executive summary shouldn't take any more than 5 minutes for someone with a great idea.

If you have a complicated business, you can start the meeting by saying—as Nashif suggests—"'It's a really complicated business, so I'm going to tell you what we're trying to accomplish at a high level.' Then you can get into the specifics around the business model or the product."

"You need to think about how are you drawing that person in and having them be part of the conversation versus just talking and talking without making a point."

And this is something Nashif knows about from firsthand experience: "I had a meeting to see if a top executive at one of Chicago's health insurance companies would invest $3 million. I kept thinking about how I could give them digestible information. As I was building and continuing to communicate, I was validating that he was still interested in what I was saying and that I was meeting his needs."

Midway through the conversation, Nashif stopped and asked, "Do you feel comfortable with the information that I'm providing? Do you feel that you have enough information to take this forward for approval to the broader executive team?"

The executive responded, "I'm understanding your business model."

Nashif replied, "You didn't answer my question. I asked if you were *comfortable* with the information I was giving you."

It might seem bold, but you need to persistently ensure that your audience is with you throughout your pitch. Without verbal or implied signs that an investor is tracking what you're saying, you can't know if you're ever going to come to an agreement. As Nashif says, "You can't adjust if you don't check in."

Long story, short. The best ideas are explained simply.

Can you summarize your big idea in a few sentences?

- Practice pitching your company's new project, goal, or mission to family members in just 5 minutes. Ask for honest feedback. Did they understand what you said?
- How can you use the BRIEF method to find clarity?

16 It's Never Really Small Talk

Simplicity is the glory of expression.

—Walt Whitman

Long story, short. Convey meaningful messages in informal, fluid settings by using as few words as possible.

Brevity as a Conversational Life Raft

The adage "Loose lips sink ships" says it all. In a time of war, seemingly harmless banter that could expose secrets to the enemy is never welcome. And the same is true in your job.

Organizations are filled with small talk and chatter before meetings, in the hallway, arriving to work, getting ready to go home, or running out to lunch. And although they seem innocuous enough, these little conversations throughout the day can speak volumes—and sink careers.

You must manage your reputation closely, and how you make small talk is one component of this. As they say in media training, "It's all on the record."

For example, I remember waiting in the reception area of Harley Davidson's corporate headquarters to visit my client early on a Monday morning. I saw a young man waiting to get signed in. He looked like a new employee on his first day on the job.

After a short time, one of the chefs walked down the hall from the cafeteria. He went up to the front desk and signed the young man in, saying, "I don't know what date it is. I'm still stuck in Sunday."

The new employee casually responded, "Yeah, I had one of those weekends, too."

I wondered, "What is his new boss thinking about him and the kind of weekend he had?" That harmless comment could imply a host of different unflattering activities, such as drinking all weekend or letting his personal life get out of control.

It's one thing to share personal anecdotes about your weekend to keep the mood light between a boss and a new employee. It's another thing to engage in familiar conversation *too* soon.

Don't let your conversation seem like business casual. If you're thoughtless with your words, your new boss will think you're thoughtless with everything else.

Momentary Misgivings Stall Momentum

Consider the case of Frank, an up-and-coming corporate star who had a bad day, said too much and stalled his career.

Frank had risen through the ranks of a top U.S. manufacturing company and was responsible for a business unit that did more than $500 million in annual revenues. He was consistently one of the organization's top performers. In fact, he could predict within 1 percent the profitability of his business unit each year. His uncanny ability to forecast and deliver revenue and profit was his hallmark.

Clearly a strong manager and an emerging leader, Frank was aggressive and ambitious and the go-to guy for delivering results and making up the slack for any underperforming units. Without a doubt, he was the guy that the organization had its eye on for bigger things.

However, it all unraveled on one fateful business trip when he and his boss were going through some intense negotiations—a stress-filled environment with high expectations for a seemingly impossible goal. Frank had known his boss for a long time. In fact, he had his current job because of him. Yet, in a span of about 5 minutes, Frank let his guard down and openly complained about the personal and professional misgivings he felt facing the daunting challenge.

His boss read his complaints as a sign of weakness and a lack of commitment. In an instant, he wondered, "Is Frank all in? Can I count on him now, or for the next big challenge?" His confidence was undermined.

A few days later, Frank realized what he'd done. His relationship with his boss changed radically over a matter of weeks. Within a few months, he was signing a separation agreement.

Frank casually talked himself out of the corner office.

You can say it's unfair, especially given all of the amazing results Frank had delivered. But people have very short memories and are quick to judge.

What you say *matters*. If it comes out of your mouth, it speaks volumes about what you can handle, and why you're the right (or wrong) fit.

[brief] BITS

Just because you think it, doesn't mean you have to say it.

Little kids and some older people have something in common: no filter. For these individuals, thinking something and saying it are synonymous. A lot of things come to mind in the midst of a conversation, but we don't need to share all of them. Think about it: How many problems or potholes could you avoid if you held your tongue more often?

When you feel bad, are having a rough day, or are frustrated, don't speak in negative headlines. Instead, say nothing. You risk delivering a dreary message that frames the situation in a poor light, and reflects badly on you and your abilities.

Here are a few things to ask yourself when you're having a tough time:

Do I pause and consider what I'm about to say before I share bad news?

Do I have a heightened awareness of the impression I give people?

Am I conscious that a negative headline I serve up can be easily misconstrued?

Do I remember that *everything*, including casual conversation, is on the record?

Walk the Walk; Talk the Talk

There's small talk like the chatter exchanged around the water cooler. And then there's small talk like the condensed briefings that fuel senators and House members as they race to and from committees, votes, and conferences.

In Washington, D.C., politics get done while walking and talking—fast. Katie knew this; she was a leadership staffer for four years and was responsible for coordinating the schedules of 55 senators.

For her, small talk meant distilling mountains of information into a few minutes. With members darting all around Congress and the country, senior staffers like to have their agendas whittled down into 5-minute increments. They're responsible for briefing their senator, or member, between meetings—sometimes with only a few minutes to download everything the senator needs for the next big vote or committee meeting.

"A staffer or multiple staffers are designated to 'pass' the member from meetings and events," Katie said. "The member's schedule is fluid, with floor votes constantly interrupting all the planned meetings and events. It's constantly changing."

To adequately brief the members in the middle of their hectic day, Katie said staffers start with a short e-mail. For the pickup, the staffer would take only a one-pager to hand the member, along with an oral briefing.

"The walk-and-talk part is often the first and only opportunity to brief them en route to the meeting. You have to take advantage of the transit time to and from floor votes in the capitol," she said. "You definitely have to be ready to go at a moment's notice."

Talk about stressful. Staffers need to keep their cool, or else. If they get nervous and start to ramble or get lost in their briefing, their member could walk into the next vote unprepared, embarrassed, and angry.

As Katie explains, it takes confidence in your preparation and knowledge to be concise. "You have to be brief. You're done in about 5 to 10 minutes," she said. "You go in the elevator from the Senate Office Building and take the capitol subway system or walk on the path along the subway system."

And time isn't the only constraint. Staffers must deliver precise briefings under intense scrutiny, sometimes in front of other senators and members within the caucus.

"I found it very hard to get used to the fact that you have to go in and brief them *anywhere*. I had to walk right up to my boss while he was sitting at the head of this big, square table during a caucus meeting. I had to whisper the briefing to him in the middle of 40-some senators," she said. "I felt really uncomfortable."

But Katie knew how crucial it was to not allow discomfort to derail any updates. Your audience, be it a senator or your manager, is counting on you to be a steady, reliable, and quick source of valuable information.

[brief] BITS

You know you've said too much when all you hear is your voice.

I asked participants in a workshop to do an active listening exercise that required a short conversation with someone. The next day, a student reported calling his wife on his mobile phone and getting disconnected. When he called her back, he knew exactly what she was saying when they got cut off because he was *actively listening*. How often do you not notice when a conversation has been cut off—and just keep on talking?

[AT EASE]

Katie explains how staffers must also tailor their briefings to each senator's expertise.

"You don't have to get into the weeds as much with them," she said. "They're experts. They just don't have any time. They have symptoms of ADD [attention-deficit disorder], because that's sort of the way they work down there."

Katie knows that if you feed your audience points that seem obvious to them, you're wasting their time. Save your breath and get to the newest, most important information in fluid, high-stress situations.

She also emphasizes the significance of listening to determine what your audience already knows or doesn't know: "You have to get a sense of what they want and what they need, as well as what they can process. They have a lot going through their minds, so you're just trying not to overload them," she said.

"They're so harried and stressed, you're literally just reminding them about the big things—who, what, when, where, and why."

Katie's team also had talking-points cards called *palm cards*. All the Republican senators got one card, which has a general message and three talking points underneath. The members were able to simply slip the week's messaging goals in their lapel pocket.

"You have to convey one major point," she said. "It's just a matter of understanding the best, most persuasive point to use—internally or externally."

You can do the same favor for your audience by cutting down your message until it can theoretically fit in the palm of their hand. As Katie explains, "It's about clarity. You might be very interested in what you're doing and prepare for it extensively. But you have to be able to step back and separate yourself—and not be so enthralled with what you're doing. You have to think of the other person, and not be too concerned about how brilliant you sound."

Long story, short. Convey meaningful messages in informal, fluid settings by using as few words as possible.

- It's easy to lose your cool in fluid or casual situations, like between meetings or in high-stress environments. Keep your wits about you.

- Become more self-aware in what you say during small talk by pausing and reevaluating what you are about to share. A good rule of thumb: if you wouldn't want your boss to overhear you, then leave it unsaid.

- Gain the confidence to be brief through preparation and practice.

17 Help Wanted: Master of Brevity

Talk to the point and stop when you have reached it.

—F. V. Irish

Long story, short. Interviews are moments to have controlled conversations, not nervous monologues.

Not the Time for Anxious Rambling

Even the most well-prepared and accomplished professionals go into job interviews nervous and self-conscious.

Brevity plays a key role during an interview. It helps you stand out clearly from the others, ask good questions, and listen.

When people get nervous, they start talking—*a lot*. If you've ever interviewed people, you can see it as they ramble on about themselves. They want to get as much information across as they possibly can.

An interview is a time for control, discipline, and awareness. Don't pour it on. Make a positive impression in the first 5 minutes. Stay in the moment, and be in a conversation.

You may be the best candidate in the world on paper. But if you're not careful in person, you can flush away everything that you've worked for.

[brief] **BITS**

Brevity is a gauge of talent.

[TOP RECRUIT!]

Unemployment is a persistent issue, especially among recent college graduates. According to global talent management expert Dorothy Dalton, brevity is the secret to a good interview. "Brevity shows that you understand the interview is about creating a dialogue," Dalton says. "It allows you to conquer nerves and facilitates strategy. If you are concise, you target your responses accordingly."

Brevity is your weapon—and it starts with the résumé. Trim it, highlight your successes, and put them in context. Don't give them five pages about your entire professional and educational history. Write a good, pointed cover letter that leaves your interviewer with that single defining idea of why you're the best fit.

Good interviews live the principles of BRIEF. You are short and to the point. You make it easy for your potential employer to understand who you are, where you've come from, and why you've been successful. You can tell your story quickly. People understand that you and your résumé are the same.

You can also sit down with someone and comfortably talk about yourself without sounding as if you're delivering a sales pitch.

You've taken time to prepare. You know to stop and ask good questions during the interview because you're listening for clues about what is important to them.

Nobody likes interviews. In fact, some interviewers do most of the talking because they're nervous, too. There's an opportunity for interviewers to be brief as well. If they can talk less, ask better questions, and be better listeners, they will get an even better gauge of the person they are interviewing.

In this chapter, I'll explore those moments when you can be much more mindful of brevity—ensuring that you get your dream job or that your position gets filled with just the right person.

[brief] **BITS**

Asking a really good question is a great way to be brief.

[OVER!]

An effective way to speak less is to act like a journalist. Seasoned Chicago radio news reporter Charlie Meyerson suggests that we view a conversation as an interview: "Do your homework. Have an idea in advance of what you hope to get out of it—even though good interviews often reveal things you didn't expect. Be ready to listen for answers that open your eyes to questions you hadn't planned to ask."

Let Others Lead the Conversation

As we've discussed, brevity plays a big role in business, particularly when trying to get your foot in the door. People tend to make some common mistakes in terms of being brief while interviewing, on both sides of the table.

A close friend of mine, Doug Hinderer, is the head of human resources at the National Association of Realtors (NAR). He's spent more than 20 years as a senior leader at the helm of an organization that certifies millions of real estate professionals as Realtors, the official designation of an NAR member.

Visually stand out

► If a picture is worth a thousand words, imagine how much you can say with a video.

Over the course of his tenure, he has seen it all.

"The most common mistake a candidate makes in an interview is talking too much," he observes. "A trained, skilled interviewer is usually very good at using silence—[and it can make] candidates very uncomfortable if the interviewer isn't firing questions back. More often than not, they find a way to step into it and make a big mistake to keep talking and talking and talking."

According to Doug, it's just a matter of time until an undisciplined interviewee either says something stupid or reveals too much information.

"When I talk to people about how to interview for a job, I tell them to look at it like a tennis match. The interviewer is going to serve up a question. Respond to it, be done with it, and wait for the next question."

Being brief during an interview demonstrates that you are a disciplined communicator and a team player.

Talking Your Way out of a Job Offer

It's painful to hear but true; great candidates often talk their way out of a perfect position.

Tom Earnhardt, a close friend and accomplished officer at Joint Special Operations Command at Fort Bragg, North Carolina, was once interviewing candidates for a vacant position in his department.

One woman came highly recommended by one of Earnhardt's previous supervisors. She had endorsements from many influential people in the department.

Her screening went perfectly. She aced a series of psychological tests, a thorough background check, and physical training tests. She had all of the prerequisites. Everyone was in her corner. Basically, all she had to do was go through the interview, and she had the job.

"We interviewed one female candidate and one male candidate in order to be fair, even though we knew walking in the door we were planning on hiring her," Earnhardt said.

The woman came in, sat down, and they began to talk. "Right out of the gate her answers were fine," Earnhardt said.

And then someone asked her, "Why do you want to work here?"

She replied, "I think this would be a very beneficial step to help round me out as a leader."

Her answer made Earnhardt pause.

"We all were a bit taken back by that," Earnhardt said. "You're in our department because you want to be here, to be part of this team."

That response led to another round of questions. The more the panel asked about her reason for applying for the job, the more fixated on herself she became.

"It was a spiral effect," Earnhardt said. "She began to talk about herself and her aspirations. She expected to be on the battalion command list in a number of years, so this would be only a two-year commitment.

"The fascinating part was she didn't realize it. Her answers were leading to more questions that she perceived as interest in her."

The panel then specifically asked about her jobs while she was deployed in Iraq and Afghanistan.

"In an organization like ours, the last thing an applicant wants people to start doing in that sort of setting is digging," Earnhardt told me. "And she was consistently in supervisory jobs rather than in practice jobs. We began to discover no one had ever put her in a job where she actually had to practice her art."

This is a perfect example of an undisciplined interviewee who failed to guide the conversation down the right path.

"She completely misread the audience and perceived that we were more interested than alarmed," Earnhardt said. "Probably the best thing she could've done was shut up, because frankly, she had the job. All she had to do was walk in there and not drop a hand grenade in the room."

Finally, the panel sent her to a waiting room. They told her, "We've got one more interview to conduct, and then we'll let you know."

The male applicant's appearance was not what one would expect for someone applying for a job in Earnhardt's command. It became clear as soon as he began to answer questions, however, that he understood not only the organization but also its critical mission better than the first candidate.

"We could see the tide turning very quickly," Earnhardt said. "I'd never had this happen to me before—had someone who came so highly recommended completely reverse me, and someone who I was predisposed to not want turn me around."

They hired the second candidate, who is now the chief of the directorate.

All business professionals can learn from this interviewee's mistakes.

"Know your audience when you're briefing," Earnhardt says. "That applicant didn't realize the level of expertise that was sitting across the table. She had no grasp of the commitment expected to the command. She didn't understand her audience, and she talked too much."

Interviews aren't supposed to be monologues. They're dialogues. Engage in give-and-take conversations.

Long story, short. Interviews are moments to have controlled conversations, not nervous monologues.

By applying brevity to an interview—regardless of what side of the table you're on—you'll be seen as a professional team player that practices discipline and self-control. Here are a few considerations to prepare for an interview:

For the Candidate:

- Be prepared. Create a BRIEF Map that quickly explains why you're qualified.

- Tell a story. Have a few snapshots of successes that you can share.

- Keep it conversational. Listen closely, ask good questions, and make sure it's a balanced dialogue.

For the Interviewer:

- Listen closely. Notice how the candidate's Elusive 600 might be leaking and what it tells—positively or negatively—about him or her.

- Sandwich the better questions. Put the meat of the interview into the middle so you're more comfortable and you are not rushing at the end.

- Don't sell. If you believe the candidate is strong, don't start hyping the benefits of the opportunity.

18 I've Got Some Good News

First the doctor told me the good news: I was going to have a disease named after me.

—Steve Martin

Long story, short. Sharing good news briefly highlights the success and leaves people wanting to hear more.

Pay the Favor of Brevity Forward

It may seem surprising that there is a chapter in BRIEF about sharing good news. Certainly brevity applies to bad news. But why do we have to exercise brevity when sharing good news?

Everybody loves to hear something positive. But consider that your role is to deliver the headline and let it sink in, not pile it on.

Those moments when you share a success story or an accomplishment need to put you and your company in a positive light. Especially in these instances, discipline and choice details give people a good impression without making them feel as though you're bragging or overconfident.

It's a time for clarity and humility.

Let the Brilliance Shine Through

Coming up with a new product idea is a great moment to spread some good news. Just be careful to be *clear*.

Bruce Smith is a top designer for the global office furniture company Steelcase. After 27 years at the company, Smith knows that having a good design idea doesn't always mean that others will get it. And when the design team sought to create something top of the line and tech savvy, like their new chair, Gesture, they need to communicate the big ideas behind the design direction clearly and quickly.

But with all of the research and testing that goes into making some of the most elegant and efficient chairs on the market, Smith and team encountered challenges in narrowing down the team's message. The sheer amount of research available to the team was daunting. And with all these data points and reports, it was critical to express a resulting singular concept.

"We would ultimately focus on some pretty simple ideas as key to the design problem," Smith said. "But the process of refining our thinking, to grasp what we were trying to accomplish was messy, and until complete, difficult for others to rally around."

The team determined that the physical postures adopted by people at work were the most concise expression of new behaviors. So they began to sort and categorize thousands of images of people at work interacting with new technology.

The result of this work was a 'taxonomy' of posture—30 simple images of people at work, 30 postures—that "sum-totaled itself in one simple page," Smith said. "We could have told a lengthy story about all kinds of significant changes."

So they packaged their findings in a clean chart: a simple, abstract diagram, a cartoon of sorts that showed 30 different postures. They turned good ideas into a clear picture.

"All we had to say was this: 'Technology, along with a new demographic in the workplace, is changing our behaviors, and here's the output: this little chart of 30 postures.' And boom. People just got it," Smith said. "It was beautiful."

Smith said Steelcase's design briefs have shifted away from a dissertation format to a cartoon-book style: "We're using words, stories, and cartoons to make what might be complex, simple and tangible."

Briefly telling Gesture's story means Steelcase did all the work to make its new product great news—and make sure the key audiences readily understood it. Steelcase's ideas have always been well researched and well documented; now, the company is just more discerning about how simply it is explained.

What's more, making ideas tangible is crucial *especially* if they are complex. Smith said getting the message into others' hands is often problematic; it can be like the "telephone game," in which a line of people whisper a phrase in each other's ears and end up with a radically and hilariously different message at the other end.

"Regardless of how simple and how clear you make the message, there's always the opportunity for it to be distorted," Smith says. "The chances of that happening go up dramatically when your message isn't brief, simple, and understandable."

Ensure that your ideas are clear enough that they don't get lost in translation when it's time to pass them along.

If you fail to do this, says Smith, "It's likely that you yourself don't have a clear understanding of your idea or goal–and that the idea will not communicate well and may fall apart out of your control. But if you're diligent and disciplined, you have an opportunity to clarify a message."

Speak the Language of Success

David Meerman Scott is an international marketing strategist for technology companies like HubSpot and GrabCAD. Author of the revolutionary best seller *The New Rules of Marketing & PR*, Scott redefined how businesses share their success stories.

"The new rules of marketing and PR are to create great content on the Web and that serves to generate attention," Scott said. "You've got to pick and choose the best way to deliver content, whether it's a very brief version or whether [someone wants] to go with long-form content."

Unfortunately for most businesses, telling the stories of their success gets lost in translation. They choose to speak an unintelligible language that is more confusing than compelling.

"It tends to be just the same words that everybody else uses, to the point where that those words like 'innovative' or 'cutting-edge' are just completely meaningless," Scott said.

Being creative with your content is vital, yet Scott aptly warns against letting your ideas wander too far from the main point. Analogies can help simplify your idea—*if* they accurately reflect your core message. Otherwise, "all these metaphors do nothing but confuse people so that the message doesn't get across," Scott says.

The PR and marketing material that clogs up the airwaves today is largely ineffective, because companies aren't doing their research. Failing to study your customers is like shooting arrows without a target.

"They don't understand their marketplace [or] their potential customers. [So] they end up taking product-based information and making it sound important with this gobbledy-gook language," Scott says.

Scott has angled the language at HubSpot to talk directly to the company's target audience. This keeps their brief message from getting lost in unfamiliar terms or turns of phrase.

"They're communicating in the language of the people they are trying to reach," Scott explains. "They're using the journalistic technique of understanding their audience. Some organizations muck up their communications with words that vaguely sound impressive and important. But at a company like HubSpot, all of the marketing people are required to constantly be in the marketplace, talking to people, whether it's on the phone or electronically and through social networks. So they're not *guessing* the language that the market uses," Scott said. "They're communicating like human beings—because when human beings have a conversation, they don't use that impressive, overused language."

Get into the Habit of Saying, "Thank You"

Brevity plays an important role when expressing gratitude. When you're thanking people for what they've done and highlighting their successes and accomplishments, give them the chance to enjoy the spotlight. Let them enjoy the moment of a short and sweet thank you.

It's about them, not about you. Say it and let them enjoy it.

End your speech early and leave them wanting more.

P. T. Barnum and Walt Disney are often attributed to the famous saying "Always leave them wanting more." The wisdom is clear from an entertainment perspective, but the lesson also carries over to business: see your communication as a performance. Executive communications coach Jeff Berkson says, "All business is a form of acting. Don't overdo it."

[OVER AND OUT!]

Taking out a pen and a card to send a person a thank-you note, for instance, is an age-old practice that many people have abandoned. But it's a great opportunity to be authentic. You can say things from the heart by just jotting a few poignant lines of gratitude. People love getting a short note that's personal and real.

Look for moments to share good news and thank others for the good work that they do. It's the hallmark of any successful executive; after all, no one succeeds by themselves.

An executive told me that the best people he's ever met in his career—the highly successful people—always take time to praise others thoughtfully.

Long story, short. Sharing good news briefly highlights the success and leaves people wanting to hear more.

19 And the Bad News Is ...

The bad news motivated the drill instructors that much more.

—R. Lee Ermey

Long story, short. Delivering bad news is a matter of mastering and minimizing a moment.

The Bright (and Brief) Side of Bearing Bad News

If it's hard to give someone bad news, don't make it harder by dragging it out.

Nobody wants to be the bearer of bad news—whether telling your boss the project is going to be late, telling your significant other you've bounced a check, sharing negative feedback from your most important client, or having the unfortunate responsibility of having to fire somebody. In all of these moments, taking the time to prepare and get to the core of the issue quickly will make the pill easier to swallow.

Remember, there's almost always a silver lining. No matter how dire the situation looks, we're never really doomed. Yet, belaboring a point will make what's painful, unbearable.

I remember early in my career suffering a major setback in
finalizing a contract with an important client. At the last moment,
the client decided to cancel the agreement, saying that he didn't
really remember approving it.

[brief] BITS

Stop talking and let people process.

[HALT!]

When sharing an idea, let people take time for it to
sink in. After presenting them with complex or large
amounts of information, give them a moment to
absorb it all. Knowing when to take a break is just
as important as setting up the idea. The mind is a
processor, and if you keep hitting the Send button,
the effect can be maddening and futile.

I nearly panicked.

That was clearly bad news. I had to call my boss and tell him
about this major setback.

My boss came to the client's office, rectified the situation, and
set the deal straight. He pulled me aside afterward and said, "Listen, kid, don't ever let it get to you."

What I took away from those words of encouragement was
that you can deal with the problem, find a bright side, and take
away some benefit.

In this chapter, we will look at how to make sure that the bad
news is delivered in the most professional, respectful, and humane
way—and that it never capsizes our ship.

Give It to Them Straight

John Challenger is CEO of Challenger, Gray and Christmas,
a recognized leader in workplace economics, labor, and

hiring. His company often counsels executives that are part of corporate downsizing. According to Challenger, in these instances, it's easy to let tough discussions get out of hand.

The best way to terminate someone's employment is to give that person the news straight and then get out of the picture so he or she can begin to process.

"When they hear the news, the blood rushes to their head and they just can't think at all. Something really bad has happened to them," Challenger said. "It is so important that it be brief. It should take 5 or 10 minutes."

In a termination discussion, Challenger said it's important to be frank and positive without being patronizing.

"In these situations, it's difficult to stay in the moment, be calm, really hear the other person, their reactions, and get on their wavelength. These situations are inherently stressful," he said. "I know people who can't sleep the night before, who sweat out their shirts."

Don't give into the temptation to overexplain in order to compensate for the bad news.

"The meeting should be focused on delivering the information. The boss is not the person to give that person a lot of comfort, because he or she made the decision," he said. "It should be done with humanity, with kindness, but it's also easy to get caught up and try to become that person's friend."

Even though you might be tempted to rehash your justifications for your decision, all they will hear is that they're not good enough.

"You don't want it to turn into an argument," he said. "This is not the time to go back over that kind of information or to berate the person."

"This should be a moment for you to deliver a little advice and a strong, short message—'You will survive.'"

"I can remember one instance where I was in the office, and all of a sudden, I heard the two people come out, screaming at each other at the top of their lungs, just in a furious argument," he said. "They were basically marched out the door. It's just volatile emotionally."

Be direct. Deliver the bad news in a kind, humane, but firm way. You have to talk about the details, but it's not a time to get into a long discussion that could lead to a stressful, unnecessary dispute.

If you have the unfortunate responsibility to fire someone, consider these three things:

- Avoid lengthy discussions.
- Keep it short. Realize that the person will need time to process after you've delivered the bad news; don't try to have the person understand on the spot.
- Doors close all the time. Help those who hear bad news recognize the moment and then focus their energy on rebuilding.

Serving up the S#&$ Sandwich

Angelo is an overachiever who is always looking for what's next. A rising star at Zebra Technologies, a growing tech firm in Chicago, he was always looking for the next career opportunity.

When a new sales manager position opened up, he was ready. But he definitely wasn't ready for the surprise he found at the interview.

"I applied for the job and got the interview," he said. "I thought it was a great sign and I definitely thought I was the most qualified person."

Angelo had the interview with the vice president (VP) of sales. He called Angelo in to his office and asked him to make himself comfortable.

What happened next changed everything.

He said, "You must be a little nervous about the interview."

"A little," he replied.

"Well, I am going to make it easy on you. You didn't get the job."

Angelo was a little stunned. Before he could reply, the VP said, "Hopefully you feel more relaxed, because now you have nothing to lose."

"Okay, I guess," Angelo said, unsure of what was to come next.

"But what we're going to do now is take this opportunity and get you prepared for the job," the VP said. "Right now, you don't have any management experience, you never formally led in a corporation, and you haven't demonstrated you have those skills. I'm going to help you create a plan to do that."

The conversation lasted an hour.

"It was really positive because he didn't serve me a s#&* sandwich. He was straight with me."

A s#&* sandwich is how most people deliver bad news or harsh feedback. They bury the bad news in between meaningless or downright disingenuous positive verbiage.

It goes something like this:

"You're a strong player, and everyone loves your work ethic and attitude, blah, blah, blah. But you don't have a clue about the project you're working on, and the wheels are coming off. We know that you have a bright future here, and we value your commitment to the firm."

Roger Schwarz, who wrote a *Harvard Business Review* blog against "the sandwich strategy," recommends that executives take a transparent approach to help both their audience and themselves.

Delivering transparent negative feedback communicates authenticity and diminishes everyone's anxiety.

People often get the good-bad-good-news combo. The problem with this approach is that it is confusing or even misleading. You run the risk of people missing the point, which is unfair and ineffective.

Imagine a thousand managers across a business serving up these sandwiches. Picture the organizational cost of all of those employees not knowing where they stand and what they can do to be better.

When giving tough feedback, give it to people straight. Those moments can be defining for them and for you.

When delivering feedback or bad news, consider three important issues:

- *Problems*: Do I state the bad news simply and clearly, not pulling punches?
- *Causes*: Do I state the real reasons why this is the case so people know why?
- *Possibility*: Can I take advantage of a tough talk to create a heart-to-heart?

It's about having integrity. Being brief is your best bet to being honest.

What's more, it could start a conversation that turns things around in the same way it did for Angelo. A few months later he became sales manager because he was ready; three years later he was manager of the year for the entire company.

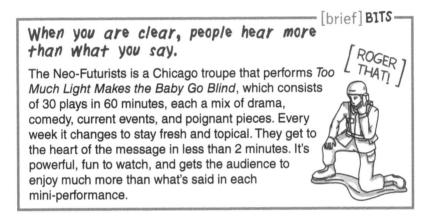

[brief] **BITS**

When you are clear, people hear more than what you say.

The Neo-Futurists is a Chicago troupe that performs *Too Much Light Makes the Baby Go Blind*, which consists of 30 plays in 60 minutes, each a mix of drama, comedy, current events, and poignant pieces. Every week it changes to stay fresh and topical. They get to the heart of the message in less than 2 minutes. It's powerful, fun to watch, and gets the audience to enjoy much more than what's said in each mini-performance.

[ROGER THAT!]

Long story, short. Delivering bad news is a matter of mastering and minimizing a moment.

20 Got-a-Minute Updates

I love deadlines. I like the whooshing sound they make as they fly by.

—Douglas Adams

Long story, short. Tighten your message to be sure your audience stays positive and on track.

The "Say-Do" Ratio

When someone asks you, "How's it going?" be ready to give a straight answer.

Everyone needs to give superiors updates. It's a part of our daily reality. Typically, we give these progress reports on the go. People stop by the office, shoot off an e-mail, bump into each other in the hallway, or pick up the phone and call.

These are moments when it's vital to paint a clear picture.

Years ago, I worked in a PR agency and managed a large team. Each member was responsible for generating media coverage for our clients.

One of my constant concerns was letting clients know how we could generate prominent press coverage. In PR, it's difficult to get a notable media outlet like CNN, the *Wall Street Journal*, or

Forbes to write about your client. You've constantly got to be looking for news hooks, story angles, and reasons for them to cover what you think is worth their time and consideration. There's a lot of groundwork necessary to generate that kind of result: building lists, researching what the news outlets cover, understanding what they anticipate in covering, understanding the news cycles, or identifying people within the organization that are qualified to speak to the media.

So when I would walk the halls or check on my staff, I would always ask people, "How's it going with the media?" Many of them would rattle off a list of activities to get their client on the radar of a prominent reporter. But one guy I worked with, Dave, understood what I was really looking for when I asked that question. In one instance, we were at a particularly important juncture with a key client that had very high expectations.

I bumped into him in the hallway, and I asked him "How's it going?" His response was, "I got nothing."

I knew that when he answered he wasn't saying, "I've *done* nothing." He was saying, "I've got nothing to report in terms of a media result for this client. I can tell you all day long what I'm doing, but you don't care about that. You want to know: What have I been able to accomplish?"

And he was right. That's exactly what I wanted to know.

If you are giving people progress reports, being brief requires that you give them *what they are looking for*—not all of the other details and information they really don't care about. They want to know about what *result* you are driving. Some people refer to this as the say-do ratio: the relationship between what you say and what you do.

My daughter Monica did an internship during her junior year abroad in Brazil. She worked for a start-up that was very similar to a Staples or an OfficeMax online. "I've discovered that it's really important for me to say less and do more than to overpromise and underdeliver," she said. "I can have all these ideas of things I want to accomplish, and I can talk all about it—but I'm only able to *do* one or two of them," she explained.

Monica told me that it was always better if she said less about what her plans were and instead *showed* her progress by doing more.

"When I started to do that, I got a lot more work, responsibility, and recognition." By taking the initiative instead of talking up her plans, Monica got her ratio in the right proportion.

When it comes to progress reports, it's better for you to get to the point. Just say, "This is what I'm doing; this is what I am getting done." Then you can have the results speak for themselves.

Be Prepared to Be Lean and Drive Out Wasteful Words

Dan Ariens, CEO of the lead manufacturer of lawn mowers and snow blowers Ariens Company, summarizes each of his company's machines and administrative processes in one page. The 8 1/2- by 11-inch sheets of paper include a simple picture, up to 10 explanatory steps, and a few comments—and that's it.

His firm has embraced the practices of Lean Six Sigma that result in eliminating waste in organizations. For Ariens, this approach also requires engaging in lean communication.

The impact of BRIEF

► Less is more.

"Whether I'm completing payroll or doing human resources or manufacturing in an assembly, there are work instructions," Ariens said. "We boil that down to one page that says, 'These are the standard ways that we do payroll, or accounting, or assembly station four.' It's very brief, very concise, and very focused work instruction."

If someone wants to amend a Standard Work sheet, that person documents his or her comments on one page as well: "Draw us a picture, give us a sentence. I take it to the supervisor for approval. That gets updated, and we've made our change. We can do that in an hour," he said. "It's using pictures and simple words and short sentences. Don't write me a big book on why you want to make one change."

Short sentences keep Ariens up to date on daily operations at the manufacturing level.

"I can walk through our plant and read at each line, handwritten, whether or not that line is producing at its regulated expected time," Ariens said. "Handwritten stuff works. It's quick; it's easy. Having someone write it down requires them to know, hour by hour, how we're performing at an assembly cell."

——————————————— [brief] BITS ——

To be succinct is the primary skill of productive professionals.

[BULL'S-EYE!]

Brevity is a force that wages battle against the constant threat of inattention, interruption, information, and impatience. Win this war by surrounding yourself with people who not only recognize the challenges of the inattention economy but also arm themselves to win it.

Keeping operative instructions down to one page helps everyone understand what's expected of him or her and what needs to be done to change it. Ariens also practices what he preaches in his own office.

"In my office, I have a single page for each strategic initiative. It states the strategy, its reason, and its purpose—and it should be only a sentence or two."

Ariens's strict adherence to brevity means he has a low tolerance for unprepared direct reports. He complained that his usual meetings are defined by agendas that are too long and filled with boisterous pontificators who tend to repeat themselves.

"It just is very wasteful," Ariens says. He can tell whether someone is unprepared within the opening paragraph or sentence. "It is really about giving concise and consistent instruction or working on a problem in a focused manner."

Ariens identified two mistakes that cause meetings to drag: "If people are insecure about their position, they keep searching for the answer as they're talking," he explains. "They're looking for people who will give them some consensus, and they'll keep going until they find people who nod their head and agree. A more confident person will get right to the point," he said.

Think of your meetings as a one-pager. No one wants to hear you go on and on.

Ariens also blames office politics for seemingly endless and pointless meetings: "People want to make sure that the layers of management are hearing them. They think they will sway opinions and take a leadership position because they own the floor."

[brief] BASICS

FLAGGING:
THE POWER OF THREES

Flagging is simply calling out the number of key ideas you want to share.

Earlier in my career, one of my mentors was a highly accomplished and humble retired journalist—a wonderful combination for learning.

While we were preparing a client for an important East Coast media tour, he and I gathered to advise her on back-to-back interviews with major news outlets. One of his key recommendations to her was that any reporter would start taking notes or take notice if you **"flagged"** your message.

Flagging simply involved **calling out** the number of key ideas you want to share. My mentor told the client how magical it was to see a reporter engage as soon as she said, "The three most important things to know are ..."

This is a powerful way to grab and hold people's attention: organize and deliver information filtered down to a **short list.**

Implications:

► **Establish logic and simplicity.** It makes it easier for both you and the audience to stay on track.

► **Provide balance and order.** There is a clear expectation of how much they need to listen and how you are progressing.

► **Keep them connected.** The audience stays engaged because they know where they are, like chapters in a book.

"It's very frustrating. You want to say, 'Okay, I got it, I got it,' and ask, 'Can we move on?' or 'Can I hear from someone else?' And when you try and push back with some questions or ask for data, people ramble on with an answer that doesn't really give you what you want.

"My most important commodity is my time," Ariens said. "If you treat it badly, I'm going to get a little upset."

The Most Important Question: Why Am I Here?

For the past several years, Jim Metcalf, CEO of USG Corporation, has required all his direct reports to state the purpose of each meeting up front.

"One day I was coming home from a day filled with meetings and I thought, 'I accomplished nothing today.' I wasn't making an impact," Metcalf said. "I was attending a lot of meetings—but halfway through all of them, I would wonder, 'Why am I here?'"

Metcalf realized that his direct reports were draining his valuable time because they simply wanted to update him, not get a decision from him. Even though they had the authority to make the call, they wasted his time by insisting on informing him face to face.

"I hate meetings," Metcalf says. "I like meeting people for a reason, but not meeting just to meet."

He prefers short meetings, and if he can get them, short summaries and no meeting at all. He expects the purpose to be clearly stated at the beginning: this is for information only or for a decision.

"I like one page. I don't always *get* one page, because that's hard for people to do," he said. "If it's more than one page, I lose interest real fast. Getting one page helps me control my time and have a greater impact on the areas where the shareholder wants me to spend my time."

Metcalf asks the same follow-up question at every meeting: "Why do you need me here?"

"I am a stickler on starting meetings on time, having an agenda. I don't think any meeting should last more than an hour. If someone is late for a meeting, I sometimes close the door—or they don't get a chair."

Having brief meetings usually requires that a member of the leadership team mediate who talks when. Metcalf usually interjects when someone is taking up too much of the allotted time. And once he's had enough of the meeting, he says thank you, stands up, and leaves. He doesn't allow anyone to take more time than necessary. Either you're brief, or he's gone.

Metcalf also manages his time when people walk into his office while he's working. He automatically begins talking to them standing up.

"If someone gets into your chair across your desk and is crossing [his or her] legs, soon you're hearing about what happened on [his or her] summer vacation," he said. "But when I'm in my zone, I'll have a brief discussion standing up. I'm escorting them out the door, and they don't even realize it."

That direct, no-nonsense approach sends a clear signal: brevity is part of the business.

Long story, short. Tighten your message to be sure your audience stays positive and on track.

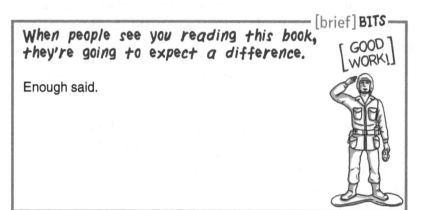

Part Four
Being BRIEF
Summary and Action Plan

L et's not forget the constant risk of reverting to bad, long-winded habits.

Since you're aiming to master the art of clear and concise communications—something others crave—we need a practical and personal plan of action to succeed. Now that you've seen the underlying whys, hows, and whens to being lean communicators, I have formulated some TIPs (truths, implications, plans/practices) to help you deliver the real impact of less is more.

Here are several BRIEF principles to keep top of mind to help you remain on track. Read them over and pick a few that catch your eye and that will have the most immediate impact on you.

1. *Your attention, please.* Manage the Elusive 600 (the excess mental capacity we all have and where inattention lives); it's your responsibility.

   a. *Truth*: We are all inundated with information and distracted easily.

   b. *Implication*: You're responsible for managing people's attention, that is, how they hear and understand you.

    c. *Plan and practice*:

       i. Watch a reality TV show for 5 minutes and write down or use a voice recorder to capture all the thoughts that race through your Elusive 600.

       ii. During the next few conversations you have, note mentally where and when people's Elusive 600 starts to leak (when it becomes too much information).

2. *Why, why, why?* Get to the reason quickly, and revisit it.

    a. *Truth*: "Why?" is the most important question that's frequently missing from our communication.

    b. *Implication*: People will never get what you're saying unless you tell them the reason it's important.

    c. *Plan and practice*:

       i. The next time you need to deliver an important e-mail, first write down the reason why it's important in one sentence—and include that in your e-mail.

       ii. Have a mental alarm that frequently goes off to remind you to say "and this is important because ...," "and that's why ...," or "the reason I am telling you this is ..."

3. *Map it out.* Prepare what you'll say on paper before you dare speak.

    a. *Truth*: The path you plan to follow must be crystal clear before starting.

    b. *Implication*: Map out a narrative flow to be sure you are clear of what level of details you need to include.

    c. *Plan and practice*:

       i. Before your next important telephone conversation, map out the three or four key ideas you want to share and how they're connected. Adhere to the map during the call.

      ii. Keep a folder of hard copy BRIEF Maps and Narrative Maps you use over the course of a month or quarter.

      iii. Map out what you have learned from this book, and use it to tell someone why and how it has helped you.

4. *Give me a headline.* Say it plainly, directly, and quickly.

  a. *Truth*: Nobody wants to expend extra energy trying to figure out what you're really trying to say.

  b. *Implication*: State up front the headline that organizes what you'll say, and then conclude with it as well.

  c. *Plan and practice*:

      i. When reading a newspaper or magazine, circle the headlines that catch your eye and write down why they appeal to you.

      ii. The next time someone asks you a typical question (for example, "How was your weekend?"), give yourself no more than 30 seconds to deliver your headline and another 30 seconds to explain why.

      iii. Read *POP!* by Sam Horn to gain deeper insight and learn how to make your ideas stand out.

5. *Take time to trim.* Just because you think it, doesn't mean you have to say it.

  a. *Truth*: An active mind shouldn't be the engine that runs a fast mouth.

  b. *Implication*: We need to be disciplined when tempted to say everything that comes to mind.

  c. *Plan and practice*:

      i. Have a conversation with a colleague or friend about his or her favorite movie or book, noting mentally how many details could be left out. Notice if you've left room for questions.

    ii. Tell two people a personal story (the best live performance you've ever seen, how you met your best friend or spouse, etc.). Share every possible detail in one, and include only the vital details in the other.

    iii. Go into your e-mail or YouTube and scan the first 20 listings you find. Note which ones are "too long; didn't read" (TL; DR) or are "too long; didn't watch" (TL; DW).

6. *Listen closely.* Active listening is vital to staying connected with your audience.

  a. *Truth*: Effective communicators need to be great listeners.

  b. *Implication*: If I listen closely, I will know what matters to others and consistently be able to manage their interest and attention.

  c. *Plan and practice*:

    i. Consider whether you can readily remember three things that seemed important after the next three meetings you attend.

    ii. Find a short YouTube video from any TED conference (www.ted.com/talks) and write down a short list of what you heard, and also what you infer from it.

7. *Just say no (to presentation mode).* Avoid speeches and monologues; always keep your information personal, professional, and conversational.

  a. *Truth*: Nobody wants to sit through a one-sided conversation and be talked at for a long time.

  b. *Implication*: Keep people actively involved any time you have to present something formally.

  c. *Plan and practice*:

    i. After a presentation, ask your audience members to write down three things they heard you say and hand them in to you. Compare their feedback with your original map.

ii. When you create a PowerPoint, include a strong visual or tell a story or anecdote on at least half the slides.

iii. Search on YouTube for a presentation on "communication effectiveness" and pick the one that looks as if it's the longest and least appealing. Watch it for its (painful) entirety.

8. *Use the power of threes*. Organize information in groups of three to keep order, attention, and balance.

   a. *Truth*: There's a reason Irish jokes have three guys and take place in a bar.

   b. *Implication*: Managing people's attention means giving them fewer moving parts to process.

   c. *Plan and practice*:

      i. Find a joke online (maybe an Irish one; clean is preferable) that has three characters and that you enjoy. Tell it to three people you know.

      ii. Think of the three most memorable things that happened on vacation or a long holiday. Write them down, and share them with someone when they ask.

9. *Cut it in half.* Whatever time you think you have, always take less.

   a. *Truth*: Busy people notice it when meetings finish early and you give them time back.

   b. *Implication*: We need to take less time than we're allotted and make it noticeable that the impact stays the same.

   c. *Plan and practice*:

      i. The next time you have a block of time on an agenda, deliver your part in 50 percent less time than you're allotted—without rushing.

    ii. Go back in your e-mail Sent folder and find a long one you've written. Edit it down to half the size.

10. *Just say it (the wrong way).* Say something simply in your own words to ensure authenticity.

    a. *Truth*: The language of business speak causes words to lose their meaning and takes too long to get to the point.

    b. *Implication*: People tune you out when you sound like the corporate wordsmith.

    c. *Plan and practice*:

        i. At home, speak as people do in meetings at work and see how your kids and family look at you strangely. At work, speak in plain English (no business buzzwords) just as you do with friends and family on the weekend.

        ii. Listen closely to how businesspeople speak, and write down words that feel like meaningless corporate speak. Develop an "off-limits" list.

        iii. Find a person whom you respect and recognize him or her in person or in writing for what he or she means to you. Don't prepare anything formal; just say what comes to your heart and mind—in less than a minute.

11. *Paint a picture.* Share a story, analogy, or even a hypothetical example to help people visualize what you mean.

    a. *Truth*: Most people nowadays are visual thinkers.

    b. *Implication*: We need to provide some creative visual element that helps illustrate our point.

    c. *Plan and practice*:

        i. Open every meeting or presentation with a short story or anecdote.

        ii. Read *Back of the Napkin* by Dan Roam for deeper insight on how to use pictures or diagrams.

     iii. Read *Presentation Zen* by Garr Reynolds for broader treatment on how to improve your use of PowerPoint.

12. *Pause, please.* Stop talking to allow room for a response, comment, or question.

   a. *Truth*: People don't know when or how to stop talking, especially when there's a lot to say.

   b. *Implication*: Providing a pause not only makes it easier for others to get involved but also shows you if they're interested or tracking.

   c. *Plan and practice*:

     i. Don't be the first—or last—one to speak at your next few meetings.

     ii. If people interrupt you, let them. They're not listening anyways; they're just waiting for their turn to talk.

     iii. Don't talk through the conclusion; just stop and leave dead silence until someone speaks.

13. *Don't use notes.* Be willing to leave your prepared paperwork aside and just say what you mean to say.

   a. *Truth*: Sticking too closely to notes or slides can cause you to not be yourself and get long-winded.

   b. *Implication*: If you're not willing and able to shred your notes, you may never be clear and concise.

   c. *Plan and practice*:

     i. During a presentation, ask the group if you can skip the PowerPoint and present without it.

     ii. Prepare a BRIEF Map, commit it to memory, and use it to guide three distinct conversations with someone (coworker or client). Don't have it within arm's reach, however. Compare your debrief with your map afterward.

14. *Don't get too comfortable.* Cut it short whenever you're on a roll.

   a. *Truth*: When you start thinking that you're irresistibly interesting, it's well beyond the time to end.

   b. *Implication*: If you want to leave them wanting more, you need to say less.

   c. *Plan and practice*:

      i. Talk to someone about a personal passion or hobby of yours, but don't speak for any longer than 30 seconds without pausing and having them join in.

     ii. Watch a TED Talk video and note how long you listen before you understood the speaker's point. Notice as well where you think the speaker could have stopped.

15. *Put it on a cracker.* Don't cook up a verbal meal; first serve a short summary to test your audience's appetite.

   a. *Truth*: Quality is more valued than quantity.

   b. *Implication*: You can be certain if people are following only if they tell you so.

   c. *Plan and practice*:

      i. During your next business call, take extensive notes and prepare a BRIEF Map summary that you can deliver to someone in 2 minutes or less.

     ii. Use a Narrative Map to summarize your favorite book or movie. Use it to share the information with someone in less than 5 minutes and see if you can get him or her to read or watch it.

16. *Nobody cares unless you do.* Remind yourself that if you're not passionate, nobody else will be.

   a. *Truth*: Some of the best joke tellers start snickering in the middle of their material.

  b. *Implication*: You have to make a conscious decision to be all in.

  c. *Plan and practice*:

    i. Ask someone you work with or know personally about a favorite childhood memory, and notice how he or she gets excited telling it to you. Let the person talk as long as he or she wants.

    ii. Write a letter to the editor of a publication about a topic that you are passionate about. Map it first and keep it to fewer than 200 words. Get it published on the first attempt.

    iii. Pick up the phone and call someone that has made an impact on your career to thank him or her.

17. *Make sure no assembly is required.* Make it easy to listen and understand by giving all the essential elements logically organized.

  a. *Truth*: Nobody likes assembling toys or bikes on Christmas Eve, and people don't enjoy exerting energy assembling random words and thoughts.

  b. *Implication*: Provide the right level of detail to create the easiest possible consumption.

  c. *Plan and practice*:

    i. Make your 11th grade English teacher proud by outlining daily. Start with updates, meetings, and important e-mails.

    ii. Try to maintain only Level 1 details for a day, using Level 2 details sparingly. Avoid all Level 3 details entirely.

    iii. Watch a talk show interview and note all Level 3 details that guests include.

18. *Tell versus sell.* While people hate being sold something, they do love stories.

    a. *Truth*: Buyer's remorse happens when you fear you were convinced to do something you didn't at first understand.

    b. *Implication*: Rediscover the elements of solid storytelling and tell a story whenever possible.

    c. *Plan and practice*:

        i. Develop three success stories that explain what you and your company do, and share one the next time someone asks about your job.

        ii. Ask someone to describe his or her best and/or worst selling experience. Listen actively, map it out, and share the stories with someone else later.

19. *What's in it for me?* There always needs to be a payoff. Know what it is, and deliver it.

    a. *Truth*: It's natural to listen and constantly wonder, "How does this affect me?"

    b. *Implication*: You need to deliver a payoff like a punch line at the end or a headline at the beginning.

    c. *Plan and practice*:

        i. Tell a joke and get comfortable seeing how the punch line is felt with immediate laughter.

        ii. Always ask before writing an e-mail: what's in it for the receiver(s)? Why should he or she read this? Include that reason in the correspondence.

20. *Commit to clear and concise.* Success means deciding to be disciplined.

    a. *Truth*: Brevity shows respect and always creates a positive response.

    b. *Implication*: If you want to make a bigger impact, decide to give your audience less.

   c. *Plan and practice*:

      i. Practice, practice, practice. Embrace and write down at least three of these TIPs.

     ii. Tell people you're reading this book as a way to increase your accountability.

   iii. Be a model of BRIEF and see it spread.

Thank you for investing the time and attention to absorb the insights of BRIEF. I'm committed to seeing a shift through teaching and evangelizing what's been shared here. The impact of BRIEF starts here with you when it's lived every day.

Be better. Be brief.

RESOURCES

Horn, Sam. *POP! Create the Perfect Pitch, Title, and Tagline for Anything*. New York: Penguin, 2006.

Lankow, Jason, Josh Ritchie, and Ross Crooks. *Infographics: The Power of Visual Storytelling*. Hoboken, NJ: John Wiley & Sons, 2012.

Reynolds, Garr. *Presentation Zen: Simple Ideas on Presentation Design and Delivery*, 2nd ed. Berkeley: New Riders, 2012.

Roam, Dan. *The Back of the Napkin: Solving Problems and Selling Ideas with Pictures*, expanded ed. New York: Penguin, 2013.

Rock, David. *Your Brain at Work: Strategies for Overcoming Distraction, Regaining Focus, and Working Smarter All Day Long*. New York: HarperCollins, 2009.

Scott, David Meerman. *The New Rules of Marketing & PR: How to Use Social Media, Online Video, Mobile Applications, Blogs, News Releases, and Viral Marketing to Reach Buyers Directly*, 4th ed. Hoboken, NJ: John Wiley & Sons, 2013.

Sinek, Simon. *Start with Why: How Great Leaders Inspire Everyone to Take Action*. New York: Penguin, 2009.

Smiciklas, Mark. *The Power of Infographics: Using Pictures to Communicate and Connect with Your Audiences*. New York: Que, 2012.

Sommers, Corey, and David Jenkins, *Whiteboard Selling: Empowering Sales through Visuals*. Hoboken, NJ: John Wiley & Sons, 2013.

Strunk Jr., William, and E. B. White, *The Elements of Style*, 4th ed. New York: Longman, 1999.

NOTES

Chapter 2

1. Atlassian infographic: https://www.atlassian.com/time-wasting-at-work-infographic.

2. Mary Meeker and Liang Wu, "Internet Trends," D11 Conference, KPCB (May 29, 2013), www.kpcb.com/insights/2013-internet-trends.

3. James E. Short, Roger E. Bohn, and Chaitanya Baru, "How Much Information? 2010 Report on Enterprise Server Information." University of California, San Diego, 2012. http://hmi.ucsd.edu/pdf/HMI_2010_EnterpriseReport_Jan_2011.pdf.

4. Ibid.

5. Sara Radicati, "Email Statistics Report 2013–2017." Palo Alto: Radicati Group, 2013. http://www.radicati.com/wp/wp-content/uploads/2013/04/Email-Statistics-Report-2013-2017-Executive-Summary.pdf.

6. Oriana Bandiera, Luigi Guiso, Andrea Prat, and Raffaella Sadun. "What Do CEOs Do?" Cambridge: Harvard Business School Working Paper 11-081 (2011). www.hbs.edu/faculty/Publication%20Files/11-081.pdf.

7. Harald Weinreich, Hartmut Obendorf, Eelco Herder, and Matthias Mayer, "Not Quite the Average: An Empirical Study of Web Use," *ACM Transactions on the Web* 2, no. 1 (February 2008), article 5. https://vsis-www.informatik.uni-hamburg.de/vsis/publications/lookpub/315.

8. David Rock, *Your Brain at Work* (New York: HarperCollins, 2009). www.advancedge.com/articles/success_street_july2013_3.php.

9. Glenn Wilson, *HP Guide to Avoiding Info-Mania*. Palo Alto: Hewlett-Packard (2005). http://demo.ort.org.il/clickit2/files/forums/920455712/548653262.pdf.

10. Eyal Ophir, Clifford Nass, and Anthony D. Wagner, "Cognitive control in media multitaskers," *PNAS* 106 no. 37 (2009): 15583–15587. doi:10.1073/pnas.0903620106.

11. Ibid.

12. Gloria Mark, "The Cost of Interrupted Work: More Speed and Stress," University of California at Irvine, 2009, www.ics.uci.edu/~gmark/chi08-mark.pdf.

13. Jonathon B. Spira, "The Cost of Not Paying Attention: How Interruptions Impact Knowledge Worker Productivity," New York: Basex (2005).

14. Karen Renaud, Judith Ramsay, and Mario Hair, "'You've Got Email!' ... Shall I Deal with It Now? Electronic Mail from the Recipient's Perspective," *International Journal of Human-Computer Interaction* 21, no. 3 (2006), 313–32.

15. Chao Liu, Ryen W. White, and Susan Dumais, "Understanding Web Browsing Behaviors through Weibull Analysis of Dwell Time," *Proceedings of the 33rd International ACM SIGIR Conference on Research and Development in Information Retrieval*, 379–86. New York: ACM (2010).

16. Michael Clargo, *Meeting by Design: Harnessing the Potential of the Web to Revitalise Meetings*. Calgary, Canada: Tesseracts (2012).

17. Carmine Gallo, "How to Run a Meeting Like Google," *Bloomberg Business Week*, Sept. 26, 2006. www.businessweek.com/stories/2006-09-26/how-to-run-a-meeting-like-google.

Chapter 6

1. Chuck Frey, "Information Triage," Mind Mapping Software Blog, Dec. 18, 2008, http://mindmappingsoftwareblog.com/information-triage.

2. "Mindjet Introduces 'Propel' Channel Program for North American Partners," Mindjet, www.mindjet.com/press/releases/2013-01-15_propel_channel/.

Chapter 7

1. "STEVE JOBS—2007 iPhone Presentation," YouTube video, www.youtube.com/watch?v=c_m2F_ph_uU.

Chapter 9

1. Mark Smiciklas, *The Power of Infographics: Using Pictures to Communicate and Connect with Your Audiences* (New York: Que, 2012).

Chapter 10

1. Brad Power, "How Marketing Can Lead Process Improvement," Harvard Business Review Blog, September 6, 2011. http://blogs.hbr.org/cs/2011/09/the_role_of_the_head_of_market.html.

Chapter 11

1. Oriana Bandiera, Luigi Guiso, Andrea Prat, and Raffaella Sadun, "What Do CEOs Do?" Cambridge: Harvard Business School Working Paper 11-081 (2011). www.hbs.edu/faculty/Publication%20Files/11-081.pdf.

Chapter 12

1. Mary Meeker and Liang Wu, "Internet Trends," D11 Conference, KPCB (May 29, 2013), www.kpcb.com/insights/2013-internet-trends.

2. Michael Chui et al., "The Social Economy: Unlocking Value and Productivity through Social Technologies," McKinsey Global Institute (July 2012), www.mckinsey.com/insights/high_tech_telecoms_internet/the_social_economy.

ABOUT THE AUTHOR

Joe McCormack is on a mission to help organizations master the art of the short story. In an age of shrinking attention spans, nonstop interruptions, and floods of information, the messages business leaders send out are getting lost in a sea of words.

An experienced marketing executive, successful entrepreneur, and author, Joe is recognized for his work in narrative messaging and corporate storytelling. His passion is to tackle head-on the "less is more" mandate.

A passionate leader, he founded the BRIEF Lab in 2013 after years dedicated to developing and delivering a unique curriculum on strategic narratives for the U.S. Army Special Operations Command (Fort Bragg, North Carolina). He actively counsels military leaders and senior executives on key messaging and strategy initiatives. His clients include W. W. Grainger, Harley-Davidson, USG Corporation, BMO Harris Bank, SAP, MasterCard, Heinz, Hoffman-La Roche, and Jones Lang LaSalle.

He founded and serves as managing director and president of the Sheffield Company, an award-winning boutique agency that specializes in narrative messaging, and short-form visual storytelling production.

He also speaks at diverse industry and client forums on the topics of messaging, storytelling, change, and leadership.

Previously, he served as senior vice president of Corporate Marketing at Ketchum, a top-five marketing agency in Chicago, where he introduced new service models to enhance messaging and deepen relationships with market influencers.

He received a BA in English Literature from Loyola University of Chicago, where he graduated with honors. He is fluent in Spanish and has broad international experience.

Joe and his wife, Julie, split their time between Southern Pines, North Carolina, and Chicago, Illinois.

INDEX

A

Action plan, 207–217
Active listening, 170
    in controlled conversations, 82
    to determine interests of audience, 87
    during meetings, 116–117
    in TALC Tracks, 84–88
ADD (attention-deficit disorder), 95
ADD (awareness, discipline, and
        decisiveness), xviii
Agenda:
    for controlled conversations, 88, 90
    for meetings, 114–115
Al and Betty Story (W. W. Grainger),
        105–108, 110
Angel investors, 162
Annual reports, 98
Apple, 59–60, 98, 158
Appreciation, for brevity, 36
Approach (in Narrative Maps), 75
Ariens, Dan, 199, 201–202, 204
Ariens Company, 199
Atlassian, 15
Attention, 56
    brevity as key to capturing, 9
    and lack of buildup time, 22–24
Attention-deficit disorder (ADD), 95
Attention span, 17, 19
Audience:
    answering needs of, 149–151
    and choice of visuals, 91–92
    determining interests of, 87
    as focus of controlled conversations,
        82, 88–90
    in job interviews, 177–180
    knowing motivations of, 160
    making videos for, 99
    for PR and marketing, 186–187
    of presentations, 134
    reading body language of, 148
    tailoring idea to needs of, 161–163
    tailoring material to, 146, 148–149
    understanding of topic among, 137
    visuals preferred by, 93–94
Awareness, xviii. See also individual
        topics

B

Background, in BRIEF maps, 51–54
Bad news, 189–195
    bright side of bearing, 189–190
    delivering, 190–192
    serving s#&* sandwiches, 192–195
Barnum, P. T., 188
Barry, Dave, 113
Beginning, in BRIEF maps, 51–54
Berkson, Jeff, 188
Big idea, 153–163
    clarity of, 147
    and mixed messages, 158–159
    narratives of, 154–157
    radical focus on, 147
    tailoring, to investors' needs, 161–163
Blanchard, Kenneth, 39
Body language:
    posture, 184–185
    reading, 148
Boeing, 50
Bohn, Roger, 16
Bolding key ideas, 103
Boring Meetings Suck (Petz), 117
Borta, John, 105–108
Breaks, taking, 190
Brevity, xviii–xvii, 3–12
    conciseness vs., 10–11
    impact of, 200

Brevity, xviii–xvii, (*Continued*)
  and interruptions for executives, 5,
      7–9
  as key to capturing attention, 9
  lack of, 3–4
  light vs. deep, 11–12
  perception of, 9–10
  techniques for, 43–44
BRIEF Box, 51–53
Briefings. *See also* Military briefings
  condensed, 168–171
  congressional, 169–171
  news, 118–119
BRIEF Maps, 44–57
  and excuse-to-impact ratio, 47
  and mind mapping (visual outlining),
      49–51
  organization of, 51–52
  payoff from, 57
  using, 52–55
  and value of outlines, 47–49
Broden, Dan, 30
Brown, Adam, 130–131
Bubbl.us, 50
Buildup, lack of time for, 22–24
Bullets, 103
Business conferences, 66–67
Buzzwords, 28, 62

C
Caldwell, William B., IV, 65, 118–119
Callousness, as Capital Sin, 28–30
Campbell, Joseph, 73
Carelessness:
  as Capital Sin, 28, 32
  in small talk, 165–166
Cartavi, 158–159
CEOs (chief executive officers), 17, 113
Challenge (in Narrative Maps), 75
Challenger, John, 190–192
Challenger, Gray and Christmas,
      190–191
Checking in, 83
Chief executive officers (CEOs), 17, 113
Clargo, Michael, 21
Clarity, 161
  balancing conciseness and, 10–11
  of big idea, 147
  from brevity, 156

  from checking in, 83
  in communicating good news,
      184–186
  of company website information,
      62–63
  with outlines, 48
CogMed, 95, 96
Comfort, as Capital Sin, 28, 30–31
Commerce, evolution of, 76–77
Commitment, 109, 130
Communication(s):
  formatting written, 101, 103
  lean, 100
  military, 154–157
Compelling conversations, 10–11
Compelling stories, 60. *See also*
      Narrative storytelling
Complication, as Capital Sin, 28, 31–32
Conciseness:
  brevity vs., 10–11
  from checking in, 83
  value of, 37, 39
Conclusion, in BRIEF maps, 51, 52, 54
Condensed briefings, 168–171
Confidence:
  as Capital Sin, 27, 29
  from using outlines, 48
Conflict, in narratives, 60
Confusion:
  as Capital Sin, 28, 31
  eliminating, 136
Congressional briefings, 169–171
Context, with outlines, 48
Controlled conversations, 81–90
  focus on audience in, 88–90
  mistakes avoided by, 82
  nature of, 84
  TALC Tracks for, 84–88
Conversations:
  controlled, 81–90
  in job interviews, 174, 177
  meetings as, 118–119
  military briefings as, 120–122
  news briefings as, 118–119
  presentations vs., 39
  sales pitches as, 61, 125
  in TALC Tracks, 84–88
  uncontrolled, 82
Core presentation, in narratives, 60

Core problem, 136
Cowardice, as Capital Sin, 27–29

D
Dalton, Dorothy, 174
Death by Meeting (Lencioni), 117
Decisiveness, xviii. *See also individual topics*
Deep brevity, 11–12
Defining problems, 136
Details:
  ignoring the "why" for, 136
  unnecessary, 36
Digital media, 123–132
  brevity constraints in, 126–128
  flood of information from, 123–124, 126
  PR and marketing material in, 186–187
  social media, 90, 92, 128–131
  time spent looking at, 21
Discipline, xviii, 81. See also individual topics
Disney, Walt, 188
Distilled ideas, 144–146
Distractions:
  as annoyance, 38
  work time lost to, 20
Document formatting, 101, 103
Dominant voices, during meetings, 116–117

E
Earnhardt, Tom, 177–180
Edelman, 61
Education, verbosity and, 131
Efficiency, of meetings, 21–22, 115
The Elements of Style (William Strunk, Jr., and E. B. White), 16
Elevator speeches, 147
Eloqua, 98
Elusive 600, 6
E-mail, 16
  as interrupter, 20–21
  length of, 103
Ending, in BRIEF maps, 51, 52, 54
Energy:
  from brevity, 109
  in social media, 130
Engagement, in social media, 130, 131

Enthusiasm, 109
Episodic videos, 100
Ermey, R. Lee, 189
Essential details, 36
Excitement, 109
Excuse-to-impact ratio, 47
Executives:
  demands on, 18
  inattention in, 56
  information overload for, 14–15
  interruptions for, 5, 7–9
  managing, 8–9

F
Fables, 73
Facebook, 130, 157
Familiarity, 30
Farris, Brad, 90
Faulkner, Kristi, 144–146
Fear, 28–29
Feedback, negative, 194
Firing someone, 191–192
Flagging, 203
Focal point (in Narrative Maps), 75
Follow-up, in BRIEF maps, 51, 52, 54–55
Formats, meeting, 115–116
Formatting documents, 101, 103
Frey, Chick, 49–50
Fun, 67

G
General Electric (GE), 98
Gilbert, Elizabeth, 140
Goals:
  clarity of, 185–186
  for controlled conversations, 88
Good news, 183–188
  brevity in sharing, 183
  clarity in communicating, 184–186
  expressing gratitude, 187–188
  and language of success, 186–187
Google, 22, 97
Gratitude, expressing, 187–188
Great Depression, 96
Gross, Rich, 134–135, 137–138

H
Hair, Mario, 20–21
Harnish, Verne, xiii, 157–158
Harvard Business Review, 110

Harvey, Paul, 88
Haven, Kendall, 144
Headlines:
  early in presentations, 37
  speaking in, 22, 69
Hearing, remembering information
      from, 93
Henderson, Eric, 154–157
Hinderer, Doug, 175, 177
HMSHost, 146
Horace, 50
HubSpot, 187

I
IBM, 149, 151
Icons, 97
IDC, 109
Ideas. *See also* Big idea
  brevity as catalyst of, 154
  clarity of, 185–186
  distilled, 144–146
  flagging, 203
IKEA, 98–99
Impatience:
  defined, 14
  and mental capacity, 21–22
Inattention, 56
  challenges of, 201
  defined, 13
  and mental capacity, 17–19
Infographics, 97–99
  age of, 92
  in USA Today, 93–94
Information:
  in BRIEF maps, 51, 52, 54
  from digital media, 123–124,
      126
Information inundation:
  defined, 13
  and mental capacity, 15–17
Information overload, 4, 14–15, 89
Insight, brevity as catalyst of, 154
Integrity, 194
Intentions, in narratives, 60
Interruptions:
  defined, 14
  for executives, 5, 7–9
  frequency of, 19, 20
  and mental capacity, 17, 19–21

  time management with, 205–206
  work time lost to, 20
Interviews:
  best time to stop talking in, 30
  job, *see* Job interviews
Investors, tailoring ideas to needs of,
      161–163
Involvement, in stories, 61
Irish, F. V., 173

J
Jargon, 28
Job interviews, 173–181
  brevity in, 173–175
  conversation leadership in, 175,
      177
  as dialogues, 180
  preparing for, 180–181
  and résumé, 174
  understanding the interviewers in,
      177–180
Jobs, Steve, 59–60, 75, 158
Journalism, 69–71

K
Kelleher, Herb, 66, 67
Ketchum, 61
Key information, in BRIEF maps, 51,
      52, 54
Know-it-alls, 29
Koziarz, Paul, 158–159

L
Language:
  body, 148, 184–185
  buzzwords, 28, 62
  on company websites, 62
  jargon, 28
  meaningless words, 28
  of success, 186–187
  verb forms, 141
  visual, 94–96
  wasteful words, 199, 201–202
  wordiness, 30, 100
Lean communication, 100
Lean Six Sigma, 199
Learning styles, 93
"Less is more," 36
Light brevity, 11–12

Listening:
    active, 82, 84–88, 116–117, 170
    to focus on other person, 84
    mental capacity for, 6
    passive, 82
    and talking sticks, 117

M
Maalouf, Elie, 146, 148–149
McCormack, Monica, 199
McManus, Emily, 139–141
mCommerce, 79
The Manager's Guide to Effective Meetings
    (Streibel), 117
Mark, Gloria, 20
Martin, Steve, 183
Meaningful messages, 165
Meaningless words, 28
Meetings, 113–122
    brevity in, 119–122
    CEOs' time spent in, 17
    as conversations, 118–119
    designing, 115–116
    efficiency of, 21–22, 115
    inefficient, 202, 204
    narrative storytelling in, 67–69
    stating purpose of, 204
    time factors of, 114–115
    time management in, 205
    tyrants in, 116–117
    villains of, 113–114
Meeting by Design (Michael Clargo), 21
Memos, color-coding, 97
Mental capacity, 13–25
    and brevity as new reality, 22–24
    and Elusive 600, 6
    and impatience, 21–22
    and inattention, 17–19
    and information inundation, 15–17
    and interruptions, 19–21
Mental muscle memory, 44
Message(s):
    clarity of, 185–186
    confusion in, 32
    meaningful, 165
    mixed, 158–159
    tracking of, 83
Message maps, 64–65. *See also* Narrative
    Maps/Mapping

Metcalf, Jim, 204–205
Meyerson, Charlie, 100, 175
Military briefings:
    brevity of, 119–122, 134–135,
        137–138
    as conversations, 118–119
Military communications, narrative
    storytelling in, 154–157
Mindjet, 50
Mind mapping (visual outlining),
    49–51. *See also* BRIEF Maps
    message maps as, 64–65. *See also*
        Narrative Maps/Mapping
    Narrative Maps, 65, 75–76,
        105–108, 110
    for narrative storytelling, 64–65
Mixed messages, 158–159
Monitise, 98
Monologues, 83, 147, 148
Multitasking:
    adapting to, 9
    and attention span, 19
    and social media, 131
Myths, 73

N
NAR (National Association
    of Realtors), 175
Narrative Maps/Mapping, 65, 75–76,
    105–108, 110
Narrative storytelling, 44, 59–80
    as corporate tool vs. art form, 73
    elements of, 69–71
    in elevator speeches, 147
    by Steve Jobs, 59–60
    length of stories, 71
    in meetings, 67–69
    in military communications,
        154–157
    mind map for, 64–65
    Narrative Map for, 65, 75–76
    need for, 62–63
    persuasion vs., 61
    teaching, 73–74
    Universal Commerce, 76–80
    vital role of, 66–67
    W. W. Grainger's Al and Betty Story,
        105–108, 110
Nashif, Nina, 161–163

National Association of Realtors (NAR), 175

Navistar, 138–139

Negative feedback, 194

Neo-Futurists, 195

Neuharth, Al, 93–94

The New Rules of Marketing & PR (David Meerman Scott), 186

News apps, 94

News briefings, 118–119

News media, 93–94

Nietzsche, Friedrich, 143

Nike, 57

Numbering, in written documents, 103

O

Office politics, 202

The One Minute Manager (Kenneth Blanchard), 39

Opportunity (in Narrative Maps), 75

Organization, information, *see* Outlines

Outlines. *See also* BRIEF Maps
  immediate benefits of, 48–49
  for presentations, 138
  purpose of, 46
  value of, 47–49
  visual (mind mapping), 49–51

Overcapacity, 6

P

Palm cards, 171

Pascal, Blaise, 50, 123

Passion, 109, 137–138

Passive listening, 82

Pauses, in controlled conversations, 88

Payoff (in Narrative Maps), 75–76

Perception of brevity, 9–10

Persuasion, narrative storytelling vs., 61

Pitzer, Randy, 61

Pixar, 158

Posture, 184–185

The Power of Infographics (Mark Smiciklas), 98

PowerPoint presentations, 138–139
  cutting number of slides in, 141
  in meetings, 116
  in military briefings, 119–122
  in sales pitches, 149

using three key points instead of, 137

Preparation:
  allocating time during meetings for, 115
  to be brief, 50, 55, 102
  for job interviews, 180–181
  by outlining, 48

Presentations:
  audience's needs from, 133–141
  brevity in, 134–135, 137–138
  conversations vs., 39
  getting to the point in, 9
  lost, 72
  in narratives, 60
  PowerPoint, *see* PowerPoint presentations
  and TED talks, 139–141

prezi.com, 97

Problems, defining, 136

Productivity, meetings and, 114

Professionalism, 61

Progress reports, 198

Pulick, Mike, 107–108

Purpose, of narratives, 59

Q

Questions:
  in BRIEF maps, 51, 52, 54–55
  in controlled conversations, 84
  in job interviews, 174, 175
  pressing, 136

R

Radical focus, 147

Radicati Group, 16

Ramsay, Judith, 20–21

Reading, remembering information from, 93

Reason, in BRIEF maps, 51, 52, 54

Relevance, in BRIEF maps, 51, 52, 54

Renaud, Karen, 20–21

Respect:
  for people's time, 150
  and telling vs. selling, 61

The Rest of the Story (radio show), 88

Résumé, 174

Rock, David, 17